ONE CHOICE, CHOOSE HAPPINESS

Angela Victoria Irwin

ISBN: 1507727879
ISBN 13: 9781507727874
Library of Congress Control Number: 2015901341
CreateSpace Independent Publishing Platform
North Charleston, South Carolina

"Happiness is not something ready-made. It comes from your own actions." – Dalai Lama

My name is Angela and my happiness is very important to me. Forever the eternal optimist, and always full of faith, I believe that there is light to be exposed even in the darkest situations. I have experienced a lot in life, and I've dealt with countless challenges and hardship just like everyone else. I've admittedly made some bad decisions, and I've fallen on the ground pretty hard a few times. Still, despite what comes my way, I have learned to recognize that no matter what, there is blue sky waiting beyond the storm clouds.

I understand that it's impossible to live life, especially the tough times, with a permanent grin on your face. I don't believe in faking happiness or trying to convince myself or anyone else that I am happy. I do believe in exposing the sun in a situation; digging so deeply through the darkness until I find the light. When we search for the light, and when we make it's revelation our focus, then we find happiness. No matter how much dirt and darkness you have to dig through, I believe there is light to be found.

Happiness is important to me. As far as I know, I have one life to live on Earth, and I don't really think it would benefit anyone for me not to enjoy it. Though I can't impact every circumstance around me, and I surely can't control every outcome, I can do things in my daily life to contribute to my happiness.

I wrote this book because over time I realized that often my actions and decisions were causing or contributing to my unhappiness. When I realized that I was a consistent source of my own unhappiness, I started taking note. I have applied everything that I recommend in this book to my own life, and I actively work to improve any negative behaviors, when I fall short. I believe making these changes and keeping these things in mind will help us be happier along our journeys. The book incorporates 30 sections which are segmented by days. Feel free to follow this guide in increments of time that make sense for you.

There are many spiritual concepts in this book. Just so you know where I am coming from, I am a Christian, but I believe my source of faith is one that anyone can relate to. I do believe that there is a power greater than us, and I also believe that we have an inner voice that leads and directs us. I encourage you to approach the spirituality of this book from the direction that makes sense for you. Whether you are spiritual or not,

Christian or some other religion, the concepts are all applicable and relevant for anyone determined to choose happiness.

I sincerely hope that my journey that is shared throughout this book leads you to experience happiness more fully in your life. Thank you for allowing me to share my story with you. May the light shine brighter in your lives, and may love grow more abundantly. Be happy!

Ang

Dedication

This book is dedicated to my parents Dennis and Rea, and my grandfather James. Many thanks to my brother Dennis, and my sisters for inspiring me. Also, I couldn't have done this without the help of Chris Damico, Megan Seegert, and Chris Wilson. I love you all. More love!!!

Table of Contents

DAY 1

Just Drop it (because it doesn't actually matter).

"For every minute you are angry, you lose sixty seconds of happiness." – Author Unknown

There will never be a day that goes by where someone doesn't do something offensive or upsetting that has the ability to affect you. Offenses may be made by people who you know, people who you don't know very well, and by strangers. Sometimes the offenses are unintentional and other times they are deliberate. Regardless of the intention, cause, or motivation of the actions of others, most often the offenses that result are not significant or meaningful enough to impact your life in a major way. Insignificant events occur all the time. Let's imagine a few scenarios of daily occurrences that are likely to happen to any of us.

1. Monday someone bumps into you on the bus, and when you look up expecting an apology they look back as if you are completely crazy to expect one. With the rudest voice they can possibly muster they boldly say "Excuse you!"

2.   Tuesday at dinner at your favorite restaurant you order a salad with your steak, but instead of a salad, your server brings you fries. When you explain that you didn't want fries because you ordered a salad, he insists that you ordered fries, but he would happily bring you a salad in addition. He then rolls his eyes at you, and walks off with an attitude so large you can see it sitting on his back, waving at you.

3. Wednesday your least favorite coworker spends the first half of a meeting kissing up to your boss. For the remainder of the meeting, she asks you questions about a project in which you have had little involvement in an attempt to make you look bad in front of your boss. Later that day, you discover that she has said a few negative things that aren't true about you to several of the managers.

These scenarios are things that most of us have experienced to some extent. Some days it feels like you walk out of your front door and the universe immediately conspires against you. Everyone is working together to plot your demise! Right? Wrong! The reality is that this just isn't the case. You are human, and just as you have bad days, other people do too. And let's face it, some people are jerks. There will always be jerks. That isn't going to change.

It is up to you to treat these meaningless situations that occur on a regular basis as being as insignificant as they really are. Things that do not matter to you or have minimum significance to your life or the lives of your loved ones, should not occupy space in your thoughts or in your conversation. When we focus on the little things that don't matter in life, we lose focus on the big picture. In the grand scheme of life, who cares if someone bumped into you on the bus? And so what if your waiter screwed up your order and has a chip on his shoulder? His attitude is his issue and not yours.

As for your coworker, exerting energy toward telling your friends at work the extent of your coworker's wretchedness paints you as a negative person. Why let someone else's attitude, issue, or rudeness become your problem? You simply don't have to do it. When you blow off these minor occurrences, you free up so much space in your mind and thoughts for things that actually do matter in the grand scheme of your life.

Time is precious and many people often feel they don't have enough time. If you stop wasting time and energy to reflect upon things and people that don't matter in the big picture of your life, you'll have so much more time available for things that are of consequence in your life, like the relationships you have with your friends and family, as well as fulfilling purpose in your life. Blow off the daily insignificant occurrences and offenses that you'll continue to encounter regularly.

I am ashamed of how much of my time I've spent retelling stories about how someone I didn't know did me wrong. I wasted so much effort and energy reflecting upon how rude people were, when really the impact was minimal. If you're used to hanging on to personal offenses, letting go will initially be difficult for you, but just as with anything else in life, if you practice you'll become better at letting go.

Two habits that I try to practice when it comes to blowing off these silly little events are to chastise myself when I'm focusing too much on petty occurrences, and to reflect on the bigger picture when I find myself getting stuck on the small things. I remember a particular instance when I was heading to visit a friend out of state, and I took a wrong exit. I asked an employee at the toll stop how to get back on course. She was extremely rude to me. For a few minutes I started getting angry, but I thought to myself, "You're so stupid for getting mad about this." I didn't know the lady personally, and I surely didn't do anything to anger or offend her. Any issue or problem was solely hers. As I prepared to head down the path toward anger, I stopped myself and recognized that if I joined her I was the idiot. Why should I give up my great day to join someone who isn't happy?

It also helps me to focus on the big picture when I find myself distracted by the small things, because then I'm able to realize what really is important to me in life. I have an endless list of personal goals to achieve. Life presents enough challenges and obstacles that require our attention when it comes to fulfilling our life purpose. I really need all of my time and energy to advance in my relationships and meeting my goals. When I start to think about everything I want to do in life it gives me perspective to realize that the minor things aren't worth a second thought from me. They are simply distractions to steer me off course.

Are you the person that's still talking about what some stranger did to you a week after the fact? If you are, learn to let it go now! You will never find happiness and achieve your goals if you focus on insignificant occurrences. Save your time and energy for things that matter.

Day 1 - Happiness Takeaways:

1. Every day someone is going to do something that is rude or causes you annoyance or frustration.
2. You're human too, and you also do things that people don't like, whether they are intentional or not.
3. When you focus on things that are insignificant you waste thought space and energy that should be going toward the pursuit of healthy relationships and achieving your personal goals.
4. Don't take on other people's issues and burdens as your own.
5. No one wants to be around a negative person.
6. Seriously, just let it go.
7. Remind yourself of how silly you are behaving when you dwell on meaningless events.
8. Remember the big picture of your life and purpose.

Reflection Questions

- What percentage of your day is spent dealing with things that matter to the grand scheme of your life, vs. meaningless things?
- _____% Purpose, _____% Meaningless
- How do you feel when people disregard your feelings? Why?
- How much time do you spend telling others about insignificant or negative experiences?

- Do you ever disregard the feelings of others?
- Are you intentionally trying to offend people?
- How will you react the next time something insignificant happens?
- What steps can you take so that the next time you experience something insignificant, you don't overreact?

DAY 2

Control Your Emotions.

**"Control your emotion or it will
control you." – Author Unknown**

Imagine a weather forecast that called for rain every
Monday. As far back as you could remember not a
Monday passed without a full downpour. Knowing what
you knew about rain on Mondays, would you venture
outside without an umbrella? Would you wear flip flops
and sunglasses? If you purposely left your umbrella at
home, would you complain about being wet when you
got wet? Regardless of whether you like the rain or not,
you know to expect it every Monday. You can't stop the
rain, but you can prepare for it.

Now consider the people or situations in your life
that cause you frustration. Just as you can't stop it from
raining every Monday, you can't change people. You
can't make someone stop their behavior, and you can't
make someone be the person that you want them to be.
Given the information that you have about someone,
you should stop expecting people to behave outside of
the parameters of who they are.

Though you can't change people, you can change your own attitude and your behavior. If it's going to rain on Monday you can fully prepare yourself to properly handle the rain. Just as we established in our example that it is going to rain every Monday, at this point you might have established that someone in your life that you can't avoid is not the best person for you to be around. You just don't like them, but because of circumstance you have to be around them. Perhaps it's a coworker or an in-law, or a partner in an unhealthy relationship. Maybe they say things to annoy you. Or maybe they are a constant source of disappointment for you. Maybe they have offended you in some way. Regardless, if you already know how that person acts, does it make sense to allow everything they do to annoy you? Why do you allow them to make you so angry? Why does their continued behavior upset you every time as if it's something new that you haven't experienced before? If their behavior is constant and unchanging, and even expected, why does it have such a negative effect on you? It's going to rain every Monday!

Take responsibility for yourself and for your actions. You, and only you, have control over your emotions. Though it is going to rain on Monday, you don't have to get wet. Knowing what you know about the weather forecast, you can plan for it and face the rain with a positive attitude! You can make an effort to keep your own emotions in check. Stop letting rainy Mondays bother you. Stop giving rainy Mondays so much power in affecting your emotions. The more thought you give to their negativity, the less space and energy you have for positivity.

If you choose to be around someone that represents a rainy Monday, accept them for who they are without constantly being frustrated. Adjust your expectations to be more appropriate for that person. If you can't avoid being around that person, expect the expected. Don't allow someone in a bad place to lead you to a bad place. Instead of internalizing someone's bad behavior, reject it. I am not condoning anyone's ill behavior, but the fact is that you can't change someone, so stop trying.

I had a really mean boss a few years ago. He yelled and swore at his employees, and I am pretty confident that the more upset we became the more he enjoyed mistreating us. I needed the job at the time, and as he was my boss, I never retaliated against him. Initially his attitude took a toll on my sunny disposition. One day, I realized that working for him didn't mean that I was stupid, and an idiot, and all of the other names that he called my team. Given that everything he said about me was not true, it really was ridiculous for me to feel bad about being yelled at.

I quickly became an expert at disregarding any of his comments toward me. His life was full of anger and unhappiness while mine was full of joy and light. Allowing his behavior to steal the goodness in my life was just unfair to me. While I could never control him,

I was easily able to control my reaction to his behavior toward me. I put up a shield around my heart and emotions that became resistant to him.

In my example I couldn't distance myself from my boss, because I really needed the job at the time. I was willing to entertain his attitude out of necessity. However, there are times when people in your life cause you pain, and you can make the choice not to be around them. Creating physical distance or taking a break from talking to someone is a great way to give you time to focus on regaining your power against their behavior. Of course there are other relationships in your life that cause you pain that maybe you need to permanently sever the ties.

There are people in life that are mean and bitter. Sometimes people have reasons for their negative behavior toward you, and other times they do not. Regardless, it is up to you to control your emotions and how people affect you. You cannot let people distract you from who you are or what you represent. If I would have allowed my boss's bitterness into my own heart, what would have become of my joy and light? Do not internalize anyone's negative energy.

If you are going to be happy, you have to take hold of your emotions. If someone you know has more power over your emotions than you do, it is essential that today you take your emotions back. It can be a difficult process and it might be a struggle; after all, we are human and not robots. I am not suggesting that you live in a way that you can be unaffected by anyone. I'm also not suggesting that you pretend your feelings aren't hurt when they are. I am simply suggesting that you prepare for the same rainy Monday you have experienced and you may continue to experience.

If someone hurts you, it is okay to admit to being hurt. But it is not okay to continue living the life of a victim and giving that person ongoing power to hurt you. Wounds that are attended to heal, but wounds that continue to be exposed and injured over and over do not. Only you have the power over your emotions. Prepare for rain and you will stay dry. Whether it rains or whether the sun shines, the only thing you can control is what you wear to be best prepared for the weather. Don't be caught off guard by another rainy Monday.

Day 2 – Happiness Takeaways:

1. You can't change another person.
2. You can change your attitude, behavior, and reaction toward another person.
3. You don't have to internalize the negative energy of someone else.
4. Regain your power by being prepared and guarding your heart.
5. Distance yourself or sever ties when you can if you are being caused emotional damage.

Reflection Questions

- What regular occurrence upsets you? Who is responsible?
- Do you think they are aware that they are upsetting you?
- What steps have you taken toward communicating to them the impact of their behavior on you?
- Do you think it makes them happy to upset you?
- How can you deny them the satisfaction of upsetting you?
- If they never change, what can you do to make the time spent with them more tolerable?
- What upsetting relationship are you in that you can eliminate?
- What about your attitude can you change so that you are less impacted by the actions of others?

DAY 3

Embrace Change.

> **"He who rejects change is the architect of decay. The only human institution which rejects progress is the cemetery." – Harold Wilson**

Life is ever-changing; it is full of seasons. Change is an indicator that life is happening. The only things that don't change in life are inanimate or dead. In order to live a happier life, we must learn to embrace change. Expecting life to remain constant and resisting change is unrealistic. Sometimes situations change and lead to our discontentment because we aren't flexible enough to make adjustments. Does our lack of flexibility actually prevent change from occurring? Absolutely not!

We often have preconceived notions of what our lives should look like or how certain situations should play out for us. We may get stuck living "inside of the box" because that requires less adjustment than learning to live abstractly outside of it. Who said you have to stay at a job that doesn't make you happy or doesn't pay you enough? Who said that you have to stay in your situation just because it's comfortable and because it's familiar? Who said you have to marry and have children by a certain age?

There are three discoveries of change that impacted my life personally, and understanding them has led to living a more fulfilled life. The first discovery of change that I had to understand is that there is opportunity in change. Change represents a chance to go in a different direction, and it holds endless possibilities for our lives. People who ride the waves of change with little resistance are able to move further along because the waves are carrying them. The momentum of change can carry you further out than your efforts alone will take you.

I had an experience where I was working for a company and I was pretty comfortable in my position. I really had no desire to remain at that company for my entire career; in fact, I had a plan to move on in six months. I was pretty confident in what I would learn and achieve there in that time, and I made the decision that after six months passed I would start looking for positions on the west coast. I remember how shocked I was when I was told that my position was being eliminated. Apparently they were going to replace my job with a higher-level global position. I couldn't be too angry as I had started planning my exit strategy, but I was a little uncomfortable with the idea of implementing my six month plan so suddenly. Fortunately within a day of receiving the news, which I knew was actually really good news, I started adapting my plan. You don't always know what life is going to throw at you in your career, but if you have the right attitude, you will understand that there is an opportunity waiting to be uncovered.

Instead of mourning the loss of my job, or being angry with my situation, I simply readjusted. I decided that my energy was better spent moving forward than looking back. You can't be so committed to "your" plan because sometimes life has other plans in mind. You can't get stuck on the idea of your plan not working out. You have to stay focused on your goals and what you want to accomplish, and more often than not, the things that we hope for do not present themselves in the neat little packages that we desire or imagine. I had no doubt that I would land where I wanted in my career, because I understood that my advancement would not come if I tried to fight the change that was happening. Even though I initially was comfortable with the idea of waiting six months to make certain changes in my life, the option was presented to me six months sooner, so I took it with a smile.

My work experience has led me to understand that there is always uncertainty in Corporate America. I've worked enough to understand how often things transform, and how unpredictable work environments can be. If you share my experience and you have struggled to embrace change in your career, perhaps it is time to embrace change by becoming an entrepreneur or aligning yourself with an organization that you really believe in and support. Even so, whether you are running the show or not, "change" will find a way to impact your life. There is always opportunity in the midst of change. If you are not full of resistance, you can easily find the opportunity lurking in the core.

The second discovery of change that I've embraced is that in order to advance in life I have to change. Until I changed certain things about myself, I would continue to encounter the same sorts of situations over and over. Until I changed, I would continue to feel like a hamster running on the wheel in a cage. My life was not advancing in certain areas, and it was no one's fault but my own. My life would not develop into what I wanted until I started doing things differently.

What held me back was discipline. I am a dreamer and I have a hundred and one ideas, but when it comes to implementing ideas and doing the hard work to make my dreams a reality, I really struggled making time to do the hard work. After working all day at my corporate position, I didn't want to come home and work more for my personal gain. I wanted to have dinner with my friends and go out dancing. But until I learned to be more disciplined with my time, I would never fulfill my purpose. I had to alter the things about myself that were preventing my growth.

Finally, the last discovery of change that impacts my life is understanding that life has seasons and that nothing lasts forever, not even tough times. Change is inevitable and an indication that we are living. Just as seasons of nature change, so do seasons in your life. There was a rough stretch of life for me a few years ago. I made decisions when I was younger that I fortunately do not regret, but they led me to a period of life where I experienced an overwhelming rainy season. There were no plants growing in my garden, because the rain swept all of the seeds away. I was on the verge of believing that I would never see the sun again. Thankfully I realized that my hard times and struggles would not last forever. Eventually the sun started shining brightly, and though it has rained again in my life since, the sun always follows.

Consider life an adventure. Along your journey you will have to hike through valleys and climb to the peaks of mountains. You might have to camp out in scary places sometimes, but other times you will sleep in open fields beneath the stars. Your journey is impacted by different climates, altitudes and conditions. Through it all though, your adventure holds so much beauty and it will undoubtedly make you a better person.

If you are someone who finds it difficult to go with the flow of change, you might have to practice until you are truly comfortable. You can do so by starting a new activity in your life that puts you out of your comfort zone. Begin to do something that you have said for years you don't like to do. If you don't like to dance, take a dance lesson. If you are a picky eater, try eating foods that have not appealed to you in the past until you like one of them. Sometimes we don't have a good reason for being resistant to change, so trying things out of your comfort zone will show you that maybe you do actually like the things that previously made you uncomfortable. If you are resistant based on bad memories or experiences, it is definitely worth trying to overcome those memories. Create new memories and experiences in your life.

When you excel at riding the wave of change your life will advance beyond your expectations and it will make your adventure that much happier. You cannot live the life you were meant to live without embracing change. Change will occur as long as you are living, so stop resisting.

Day 3 – Happiness Takeaways:

1. Change is an opportunity.
2. Change is the only constant part of life.
3. Without change you can't reach your goals.
4. Your undesired circumstance has to change.
5. Become more flexible.
6. Set a goal and then ride the wave.
7. Nothing lasts forever.

Reflection Questions

- Is there an opportunity for change in your life that you have resisted?
- What changes can you make in your personal life?
- Do you embrace change?
- What do you like about change?
- What makes you resistant to change?
- Does change lead you to your goals, or prevent you from reaching your goals?
- What steps can you take to fully embrace a significant change going on in your life that is inevitable?

DAY 4

Live Fearlessly.

"Fear is the highest fence." – Dudley Nichols

Many of us live our lives under the assumption that we are not fearful people. We think fearful people are those who don't step on cracks on the sidewalk or who are germaphobes that carry disinfectants around wherever they go. We think people who ask servers in restaurants detailed questions about food preparation techniques are fearful people. Rarely do we think of ourselves as living fearfully.

I have a healthy respect for caution when it comes to danger. I will never rollerblade on a floor that was just mopped and I will probably never hike an erupting volcano (though I hiked one that had activity a few weeks after I was on it). "I don't live my life fearfully" is what I've thought about myself my entire life. I even went skydiving, which was a clear indication that I was not fearful. Until one day the light bulb came on and I was finally able to be honest with myself.

I started thinking about the fact that I never took many risks in my career or when it came to doing things to help me reach my personal dreams and goals. Sure I've pursued my dreams to an extent, but when it came time to put myself all out, I never could. I never really believed that my fallback plan, the safer plan, wasn't the best option. Though I asserted that I didn't live in fear, I always played things safely. I was never willing to "risk it all."

If you aren't afraid, then why aren't you more aggressive in going after the things that you want? If you truly are fearless, why are you waiting for things to come to you instead of venturing out to claim what you want and deserve? If you believe something is for you, why won't you ask for it, or take what you want? If you are not afraid to fail, why haven't you tried your idea yet? Why are you still just talking about your plan, and not putting it into action?

What are you afraid of? Fear comes in all forms but based on my experience the main fears that have impacted my life are:

1. Fear of not reaching your potential in your career.
2. Fear of failure in your personal relationships.
3. Fear of rejection.
4. Fear of failing to achieve your personal dreams and goals.

5. Fear of ending up like someone in your family who you don't respect.

I couldn't work to overcome my fears until I admitted that I actually was afraid. Overcoming fear is something we constantly have to work at. As you triumph over one giant, there is a larger and stronger giant waiting on the sidelines, sizing you up, that will take a different strategy to defeat you. The key to overcoming fear is knowing you can defeat any giant in your life. If you want to break out of your current mold, you can. There really aren't obstacles holding you back besides yourself and your inability to take action.

There aren't many multimillion dollar companies that started out making millions of dollars on day one. If you're fortunate to have the capital you need to start your business that is great, but if you don't, that doesn't mean that you can't begin your dream today. Is fear telling you that starting off small isn't worth it? Is fear telling you that you have to wait until you have more money? We create limits and prevent our dreams from becoming realities. Our personal fears create realities that don't have to exist.

I have a few friends who have had problems in their careers because of fear. The same is true of my own career. I have had countless conversations with friends who weren't promoted as they should have been or who didn't receive the respect or credit they deserved for their work. We would always reflect on the people that were less qualified and overall "not as cool," yet these people continued to get the positions and respect we were denied. What is different about the person who keeps getting ahead and doesn't seem to deserve advancement and you? The difference is that they aren't afraid. They aren't afraid to ask for a promotion. They aren't afraid to flaunt their stuff in front of you, the boss, or anyone else. They network with executives and form relationships with people of influence. They are very vocal about themselves and their contributions, while you take a back seat expecting your boss to notice you.

Perhaps you have excelled in your career, but your personal relationships struggle. I remember the first time I fell in love. I fell so hard and so suddenly and it was beautiful. When it ended, I was hurt, but life moved on. From that point on, every time I dated someone or became involved in a serious relationship, my family was concerned about me getting hurt again. But how enjoyable is it to live life avoiding love in order to avoid hurt? All people are different. If someone hurt you, that doesn't mean everyone will hurt you. If someone broke your heart, you shouldn't expect all people to break your heart. Living fearlessly includes living in a vulnerable way that exposes your heart. If you never open your heart you can't experience the fullness of love in the way it is intended for us to experience.

I had a boss who had every material thing in the world one could want, but he didn't trust anyone. I could never imagine how difficult it must have been to try to anticipate the next bad thing that someone would do to you. Everyone is not out to get you. Living life expecting someone to do you harm takes far more energy than giving love and expecting love to return to you.

You can reach your dream. You can achieve whatever it is you desire. You can reach any personal goal that you desire. You can overcome your past. You can be loved in a healthy relationship. You can excel and be promoted. You don't have to be afraid any longer. At this point if you still haven't admitted that fear is part of why you are not where you want to be, I encourage you to dig deeper and acknowledge it, because as long as you have fear, you have limitations.

How does one overcome this fear? For me, my faith helps me overcome. Whether you believe in creation, evolution, or anything else, you have to believe that you are not here just to exist. You are here to live life, and living doesn't constitute simply surviving, it involves thriving and shining. I believe that the universe conspires in my favor. If I don't achieve my desired goal, I am confident that my efforts will lead me down the path of something even better. Taking risks does not lead to failure in my life, because I will certainly reach the path of success and prosperity intended for me.

Until you believe that your life is meant to be rich and full of light, it will not be. I overcome fear by knowing that I have nothing to fear. In life we have to take risks, which requires venturing into the unknown. But if we believe that the universe conspires for our wellbeing, then is it really a risk? If your light leads you to an unfamiliar place, you will find happiness much faster than staying in a dark place because you are afraid to leave your comfort zone.

Verbalizing your fearlessness does not make it so. While stating it verbally may be a reminder that fearlessness is something you aspire for, your actions more clearly define whether you are fearless or not.

Ask for the raise you know you deserve or take on the project that will elevate you at work. Your boss is not superior to you, and he or she cannot intimidate you. Everyone, even those in leadership roles or in positions of authority, is human, just like you. Be the person that you are and stop dreaming about being. Just be. Accept love in your life, because love benefits your life and doesn't hurt it.

Today, I encourage you to truly embrace fearlessness. You have nothing to lose. You will never fulfill your purpose until you stop being afraid to be yourself. You are fearless. You take risks and you aggressively take action to reach your goals and realize your dreams.

Day 4 – Happiness Takeaways:

1. Your fear will hold you back from reaching your goals.
2. Admitting your fear is the first step to overcoming your fear.
3. Until you overcome your fear, you'll never be able to live up to your true potential.
4. Believe that things will work out for you.

Reflection Questions

- What are you afraid of?
- Is your fear based on an actual experience?
- What fears do you have that you haven't acknowledged before?
- Are you more afraid of taking a risk or of failing?
- Has fear caused inactivity in your life before?
- Are you satisfied with the idea of fear preventing you from accomplishing certain things in your life?
- What steps can you take to overcome one major fear in your life?

DAY 5

No Worries!

"A day of worry is more exhausting than a day of work." – John Lubbuck

I remember a time in my life when I was not exactly thrilled with how things were going. I could see where I wanted to be in life five years down the road but I couldn't quite figure out how to get there. I was so focused on how dissatisfied I was with the sluggish rate of my progress that I couldn't enjoy living my life at that moment. I felt like everything I spoke to my loved ones was misunderstood, and that it was impossible for me to share my feelings with anyone. I was at a place in my life when for the first time I was starting to really understand what I wanted out of life, and while I was growing, I felt so alone because no one could relate to where I was coming from. As I have lived my life constantly engaged with others, always having input and opinions and conversation about life, I felt really uncomfortable. I had so many conflicting emotions, and to be honest, I was not managing them well. I wouldn't admit to being depressed, but I was undoubtedly a slow and dull version of myself.

One day I couldn't stand who I was becoming emotionally. I was to the point that I was constantly up and down, one minute thrilled and excited, the next minute discouraged and sad. I had enough of myself and I decided that it was time to snap out of the funk. Even in the midst of struggle, one is not required to live in a rut, or ride a constant emotional rollercoaster. If I truly trusted that the universe would conspire in my favor, there was no need to feel sad or down or unhappy just because I wasn't where I wanted to be. I was well on my way.

Around that time, I remember coming home one day and signing on to social media and learning of the death of one of my classmates from Penn. She was a couple of years older than me. I met her before I began my first semester; I visited for a weekend during my senior year of high school, and I randomly met her. She spent time with me, sharing her experiences as a student, and providing insight into the culture and student life. I missed the weekend where the school had a formal program set up for prospective students. This girl just gave up her time expecting nothing in return, without knowing me or whether I would actually attend Penn or not. I never became best friends with her, but I always knew her and we always spoke when we saw each other in passing.

She was such a bright light. People only said good things about her. She was in her early 30s, engaged to be married, and thriving. Her last comment on Facebook was "he lives." I found out that she had a blood clot that made its way to her heart. I felt so badly for her loss, because I could only imagine what tremendous pain her family and fiancé were feeling. Her light went out from this world before she accomplished so many things that I'm sure she planned.

What a reality check. In the moment of me discovering her loss, I became so grateful for my life, the hard times and all, and I realized how limited my perspective often was. I had more than I needed, more than a lot of people in the entire world. I was so blessed and so capable, and so ashamed that my thoughts so frequently focused on me and my small fragment of the world. How much energy do we spend on our small concerns, as if our existence is the point of life? It is far easier to understand just how sensitive life is when the life of a young person is suddenly taken.

I am not implying that our daily concerns are not significant; however, we exert energy toward things that have no impact on our lives at all. We spend valuable time analyzing trivial things such as the decisions of the latest and hottest celebrity, who they are dating, and what they are wearing. We exert energy on gossiping with our coworkers or disliking our bosses, when in reality, that energy is simply wasted. I can't remember half of the people that I spent energy disliking or talking about at my first job years ago. But during the time it was all so important to me. I was so impacted by the decisions of people that shortly after leaving that job, I couldn't even remember their names and some of their faces.

Tomorrow is not promised to anyone. So why not make an effort not to waste energy while we are here? Why don't we make more of an effort to focus on things that do matter in our lives? Instead of focusing on what we don't have, or who we don't like, or who offended us, or who doesn't love us, why not focus on fulfilling purpose and loving people around us? As long as we have life, we have the chance to impact our situations and the lives of others around us.

I started saying "no worries" as second nature years ago. If someone takes the seat I was heading to on the bus, "no worries" is my natural response. If someone bumps into me in the lobby of my office building, "no worries" is what I say. If I lose my job or my home, "no worries," I will find someplace else to work and live. Life is too short to spend worrying about the things we can't control.

I had to learn to adopt a "no worries" attitude for the larger, more important things in my life. It's sort of easy to blow off relationships and situations that don't impact your future, but when there is more at stake, it is extremely difficult to set our worries aside. However, if you believe that things will work out for you regardless of what catastrophe you are experiencing, then you will be able to look past what is going on in this moment. Count your blessings even when you're living in the wilderness, because as long as you are living today, your situation has the ability to change. Worry less and act more.

Embrace a "no worries" type of life. Even in the middle of your wilderness, don't ever stop believing that things will work out for you. Whether in the desert, on the beach, in the mountains, or in the forest, things will work out in your favor. Look for what it is you can learn and ways that you can grow in situations that are less ideal for you. Be thankful for today and trust that you will end up where you are supposed to tomorrow. As long as we have life, we should be thankful for the time we have and not worry it away.

No worries.

Day 5 – Happiness Takeaways:

1. Life is meant to be lived, not worried away.
2. Most things aren't worth the effort of worrying.
3. Focus on what you do have and where you are.
4. Trust that there is a process.
5. Act more and worry less.

Reflection Questions

- What do you worry about?
- How often do your thoughts involve worries?
- Given a tough situation, do you default to worrying or having faith that things will work out?
- What steps can you take to worry less?

DAY 6

Small Beginnings Count Too.

**"From small beginnings come
great things." - Proverb**

What tasks are on your "to do" list? What has been on your list as far back as you can remember? Maybe your thought is "when I lose weight, I'll do that." Or maybe it's "when I have more money I will travel there." Perhaps it's "when I have more time I'll start a business." What is the goal, dream, or desire that has become trapped in your conversation with others, never to be fulfilled? What happens if you never lose weight, create more time in your life or save enough money?

You don't need to have all of the answers to get started, and you don't have to try to tackle everything on your "to do" list all at once. I've always had a long list, but over time, as I grow and develop, and the more I'm exposed to, the more I add to my list. Having a long list can be overwhelming, but starting is the first and most important step to crossing items off your list. Though your list grows, if you start some of the things, you at least get closer to finishing them.

What is holding you back? If you're overwhelmed because all you can see is the end of the race, take a step back. You don't have to finish the race today, you just have to start. If you never actually start the race, you most certainly can't finish it. I had a conversation with a friend who wanted to start a business but she didn't have enough money to start where she wanted. She was right. She would have had to save money for years or raise a lot of funds somehow in order to start the business that she had in mind. I asked her why she couldn't start something similar but that required less money? Why can't you create your dream within the current parameters of your life?

Starting small is a wonderful way to begin. Maybe you will have to open a lemonade stand before you open a gourmet restaurant. Perhaps you can only afford to remodel one room in your home right now, as opposed to building a brand new home. Maybe you can only take one class at a community college, instead of attending a university full time. Small steps toward a goal are still steps. Stop trying to finish the race in one minute. As the saying goes, "Rome was not built in a day." If you take the initial steps and get started, you will find that as things progress, starting was really the most challenging part.

As a child I loved to write, but I never thought of it as something I wanted to do professionally. I always considered myself as someone that should work in a corporate environment. When I think back to how

I concluded I should work in business, I realized it was really only because I think strategically and I am persuasive. As an adult, when I realized that writing was connected to my purpose, it took a while before I started writing a book. For years I sent an encouraging email to a few of my friends every Friday. After that I blogged for a while, and eventually I started writing a book. All of these steps led me to where I am now.

Before you can master anything, you first have to practice. Once you begin, making progress is extremely important. If you start but you are still talking about what you are going to do beyond taking action, you won't advance very far. As we move forward, even on small tasks, we see our progress and we become more encouraged which causes us to progress even further. As we check things off of our lists, we develop positive habits, and we learn to see things out until they are completed.

It takes approximately nine months for a baby to fully develop and be ready for birth. Though birth only takes hours, the entire process is a major one that takes a significant amount of time. Sometimes we look toward the end or the actual birth of things that we want to occur on our lists, and become overwhelmed. Of course it would be overwhelming to find out you are pregnant one day and that you had to give birth to an eight pound baby on the next day. Fortunately this isn't the case.

Before we can give birth to the things that we wish to accomplish, be them large or small goals, whether they are personal, spiritual, or career focused, we must endure a process. We often admire people who appear to have it all together. Maybe you envy a person who is financially successful. Whatever or whomever you are trying to become, you have to remember that even the person that makes it look easy went through a process before they gave birth to their dream.

Take one step at a time, and you'll find when it is time to give birth, you will be ready. There is of course another level of responsibility after giving birth to our goals and dreams. At that point, you have a new baby to parent and mentor. Take the first step, and commit to the process and you will find your list getting easier to manage. Even if your beginning is small, it is still the most critical step, so do yourself a favor, and take that initial step. You will never truly be happy until you do.

Day 6 – Happiness Takeaways:

1. You can't finish if you never begin.
2. Focus on one goal at a time.
3. Small beginnings are still beginnings
4. Rome wasn't built in a day.
5. Building is a process, not an event.

Reflection Questions

- What is one goal that is really important for you to accomplish?
- Why is this goal important to you?
- What has prevented you from completing this goal so far?
- What is your timeline for completion?
- What resources will you need to get accomplish your goal?
- What actions can you make to get started today?

DAY 7

Don't be a Control Freak.

**"Freedom from the desire for an answer
is essential to the understanding of a
problem." – Jiddu Krishnamurti**

When I was younger I could never hula-hoop. I would
try and try, and after numerous unsuccessful attempts,
I would give up. It seemed such a basic concept, yet, I
could never do it! I tried moving my waist at varying
speeds, bending my knees, standing more stiffly, as
well as using my hips more than my waist. Even as a
child I had wide hips, and I figured that my body shape
alone with certain movement should be able to sustain
a hula-hoop from falling instantly. The harder I tried,
the sooner I failed. Eventually I gave up altogether
and stayed away from hula hoops since they caused me
frustration.

Fast forward several years. My parents love to host
parties. For several years they hosted a summer party
for many of our friends and family. I created the flyer
for the event and I called it the "Annual Fun Fest"
which somehow caused my mother to freak out and

feel pressured to actually plan lots of "fun" events for the party. "You can't call it a fun fest Ang, without planning some sort of fun events," she said. A few weekends before the party, we went to the store to pick up a few games and toys to ensure that the "fun fest" was indeed a fest full of fun. At some point, we came across a shelf of hula hoops. Instinctively I picked one up, and decided to give it a go. With little thought or effort, I began to hula-hoop! I could hold that hoop up for what seemed like hours. Given that before I could never hold it for longer than a few seconds, I impressed myself with 30 seconds. My mother quickly snapped me out of my hula-hoop heaven. "Is my adult daughter really hula hooping in the aisle?" she asked.

I have so many examples of things that I really tried to force and that never happened for me until the time was right. In high school when I took dance classes my turns were terrible. Years later I started salsa dancing, and my spins actually became quite good. I've never been a great cook and my family has always hesitated to eat my food. I eventually discovered I am good at baking sweet potato pie, which my family really enjoys. I could never jump double-dutch rope, which was always a mystery to me as I am one of the most coordinated people in the world. Perhaps this isn't a great example, because as far as I know, it's still something that I can't do. But I do realize that just because I never could in the past doesn't mean that I never will be able to in the future. If it turns out that I can't, I have discovered so many other things that I'm good at doing.

What is it that you are trying to force? What are you trying to make happen in your life by applying pressure? Are you trying to get to a place in life that isn't for you, or maybe you just aren't ready for it right now? Perhaps it's a relationship and the timing is just off because you are both in different places in life. Or maybe you are an overachiever and the only reason you are trying to do something that clearly isn't working for you, is because you think you are a failure if you stop trying.

For you "hula-hooping" can be something silly like my example or it can be far more serious and major in your life. Whatever the case may be, putting something down, walking away, trying something new, or taking a break are all okay to do. You just may find that if you visit something later, you may be better at it, or you might have new ideas or a new process for how to make it work. If something isn't working it is okay to stop, or even press reset. You might also find that if you stop trying so hard to make something work, you might discover something that is more worthy of your time and energy.

In the event that you are thinking that you will never give up, back down, or quit, please believe that I'm not encouraging you to do so. I understand that practice makes perfect. I am not trying to create a following of people who give up in life. Consider pieces of a puzzle that fit together. When I was a child, I couldn't fit those pieces together to hula-hoop but as an adult I was able to do so. I don't know what changed, or why something did change, but I respect that a change transpired, obviously so, because now I can hula-hoop. However, there was nothing I could have done to fit pieces of a puzzle together that just didn't fit.

The key takeaway here is that sometimes it's not you. Sometimes there is nothing more you can do to make something turn out the way that you think it should. If it will be, it shall be. Accept it, respect it, and hula-hoop! Drop the microphone and walk off the stage. Stop trying to force things that either aren't meant to be or aren't meant to be right now. There are enough puzzles out there with pieces that will fit for you. Instead of being determined to work with the same few pieces, find another puzzle that makes more sense for you and your life right now. You can revisit that other puzzle later, or you might even find you aren't interested in it over time.

Though it might seem counterintuitive to those of us who have a tendency to be control freaks, letting go and moving on is often a fast track to happiness and living a more fulfilled life. Simply trying to control everything in life causes stress and drama, because life is not meant to be controlled. It is meant to be lived. There are factors in life that we just can't control, some of which we addressed earlier. You can't control other people, the economy, and nature among other things. If we focus our energy on living life and finding the light in our lives, then we won't have time left over to waste on trying to control everything.

Trying to have control absorbs energy that can be spent pursuing happiness and living a more pleasing life. Spend time discovering your passions in life and fitting together the right puzzle pieces. Refocus your energy toward living a life of purpose and light, and the rest will take care of itself. If you put the hula-hoop down that doesn't mean you will never hula-hoop. One day you probably will, or either you will find an activity better suited for you.

Day 7 - Happiness Takeaways:

1. You can't control everything.
2. It is okay that you can't control everything.
3. Stepping away, taking a break, or refocusing is not giving up.
4. Trying something new isn't quitting.
5. Moving on might be a better alternative than staying.
6. If the pieces aren't fitting together, get a new puzzle.

Reflection Questions

- How do you feel when you are not in control?
- How does it make you feel to lose control?
- What is the cost to you of giving up control?
- Can you be happy if you are not in control?
- Are the pieces of your puzzle fitting together?

DAY 8

Keep it in Perspective and Get Over Yourself.

"A penny will hide the biggest star in the universe if you hold it close enough to your eye." – Samuel Grafton

I want to share with you a few thoughts that I've had in the past, and maybe I'm still guilty of having sometimes today:

"I have really nice cocktail dresses, but I don't have enough casual dresses."

"My wardrobe is nice, but my accessories are so ordinary, so I need to get a few more trendy pieces."

"I look okay in my clothing, but I really need to lose 10 pounds to look amazing."

"My brother and I are close, but he really should do a better job with communicating and trying to relate to me."

"My family is always there for me, but sometimes I wish they shared more of my interests."

"I really want to go to Argentina this year, but I have to save up to buy a new car."

"I really am tired of my neighborhood, but because of this awful real estate market, I can't sell my condo."

Reading my shallow thoughts makes me ashamed. I spent a lot of time, too much time, focusing on things that I didn't have, or things that I couldn't afford, or how awesome my life would be if I could go to Buenos Aires for two weeks. No one in life has every single thing they want. It is the nature of people to always desire more, so even if you won the lottery tomorrow and you never had to work another day in your life, and you could afford to acquire anything you ever dreamed of, there is something that you would find to complain about not having that would of course in your mind, enhance your life.

Have you ever heard someone with a great body complain about being too fat or too thin? Or have you heard someone with amazing hair complain about how awful their hair is? When I think about the times when my complaints were as ridiculous as those, I become frustrated with myself. I've found myself many times in my life complaining about something work related, when in reality at the time I actually had a pretty amazing job. When I take a moment to reflect upon my complaints, I have to laugh at myself. I am no different from the person with a six pack, complaining about being out of shape!

I had a good job, yet I reflected on the things that I didn't love about it. And though I honestly didn't prefer my neighborhood, I didn't often enough reflect on the fact that I wasn't homeless nor have I ever been. There is someone out there that would be grateful just to have a home. Perspective is key. I am fully convinced that for every complaint that I have in life, and for everything that causes me to indulge in a self-pity party, that there are thousands of other people out there who have it worse than me and who would love to have what I am not satisfied with.

Sometimes we are overly self-consumed and we spend excessive amounts of time thinking about ourselves. For this, there is a simple solution, and that is to put things in perspective. Reflecting on your life and your circumstances as they relate with the rest of the world is a wonderful exercise that will lead to you getting over yourself. If you really want to live a healthy, happy, and positive life, you must learn to appreciate what you have and don't take anything for granted.

Most of us have friends, family or people that we know that are in need. Those needs may vary broadly from emotional to financial, but regardless they are important. Make a list of needs that others have, and spend some time each day focused on the needs of others. Reflect on how much you want things to work out in the lives of others. Make another list of things that you have in your life that you are extremely thankful for, and when you feel yourself losing perspective pull out that list and recognize how many reasons you have to be grateful.

The world does not revolve around one individual, and if it did, it wouldn't be you. Sorry, but seriously, get over yourself. I've gotten over myself and it's changed my life. Putting things in perspective is one of the most efficient ways to change your life. Doing this enhances humility, which is essential to strong character. If you want to advance your life, put things in perspective. Don't ever stop striving and working hard to make positive changes, but don't ever make your problems the center of your universe. You can be happier when you understand how rich and full your life already is.

Day 8 – Happiness Takeaways:

1. The world does not revolve around you.
2. Get over yourself.
3. Exert energy toward caring about others.
4. Appreciate what you do have.
5. Think about the people less fortunate than you are.
6. Focus on the needs of others.

Reflection Questions

- In what areas of do you need to expand your perspective?
- Do you have sensitivity for people who have different experiences from yours?
- Do you consider your experiences to be typical of most people?
- Do you volunteer?
- What volunteer organizations or activities can you commit to in the next month?
- How does knowing the hardships of others impact your journey?

DAY 9

Vacation Every Day.

"Laughter is an instant vacation." – Milton Berle

Every day we solve countless problems. We find resolutions for issues at work, in our personal lives, and the lives of our friends and families. We figure out how to exist among changing conditions. We adjust when we lose our jobs. We balance budgets more efficiently when our families expand. We comfort our friends when they experience loss or trauma. We live every day getting by, surviving, and existing in the world. We focus so much on maintaining and surviving that we have to plan our actual enjoyment.

We schedule vacations in order to get away, to temporarily escape from our normal lives. When I was growing up, it seemed like I would hear in church every Sunday "tomorrow is not promised." Those words didn't become reality to me, until I started experiencing death in my own life. My maternal grandmother passed away when I was six and I can't honestly say that I really understood the reality of her passing. As a teenager in high school, I remember knowing of kids that died and I thought it was awful, but it didn't hit too close to home. In college, I heard news of one of my old classmates dying in a car accident and I initially had difficulty processing her death. How could someone die so young? The first death that truly affected me was that of my uncle. He was 40 something and not ready to die.

It makes me cringe to hear people with lives that are not enviable mention that their life will be greater in heaven. I've heard this one in church a million times as well. Don't get me wrong; I believe in heaven, and I believe that our lives here can't compare to what life in heaven will be like. However, knowing God as I do, I can't honestly believe that his intention of creating us in the first place was for us to live without any sort of enjoyment or appreciation for living on Earth.

Do you ever take a moment to slowly inhale and exhale; simply to appreciate the wonder of breathing? When I really think about how awesome the human body is, from the complexity of cells and how the body is assembled to perform as an efficient machine, it amazes me. The first time I took bikram yoga and did the opening breathing exercise I was amazed and surprised at the capacity of my lungs. When I look at flower petals, blades of grass, or cloud formations and truly reflect on their existence, it overwhelms me. Even if you don't believe in God; if you view everything from a scientific point of view, it is no less remarkable.

We are surrounded by beauty and greatness, yet, we spend the majority of our lives trudging along day-to-day, focused so much on the "business" of it all. We aren't here just to exist, we are here to live; to truly appreciate and benefit from all of the wonders of life. Why do we have to schedule time twice a year to "vacation?" Why can't we spend every day of our lives in a perpetual state of appreciation and awe that brings relief from the monotony of our bland routines?

Life is meant to be lived. We are not here to pass the days. We are here to be at one with the world and truly enjoy all that it has to offer. What will it take for you to get beyond the business of your life? What will it take for you to invest in the enjoyment of your life? Taking a vacation is like only taking care of the leaves of a plant. Without addressing the root of our issues in our lives we will never have healthy and flourishing plants. The best way to live our lives is not by simply hanging on by a thread until our next vacation. We must make enjoying the daily aspects of our lives a priority. Life is too short to only enjoy it twice a year.

I used to be a person who lived for the weekends. I would wake up Friday feeling as though I had been given the greatest gift ever. I spent all of Friday sharing my love and joy for life with everyone around me. I was practically hugging and high fiving every person I encountered. One of my friends thought it was both hilarious and slightly annoying. By Sunday night I was sad to go to sleep because I knew that when I woke up it would be Monday, and Monday meant another work week; another week for me to sit at my desk all day and not spend my time doing the things that I truly enjoyed. Instead of living for the weekend, I had to start living for every day, as each new day holds beauty and light that is meant for me to enjoy.

How do you actually feel when you are on vacation? What can you do in life to produce similar feelings? Start incorporating things into your life that allow you to enjoy yourself and actually capture the same feelings and energy you feel when you are on vacation. For me it's dancing; when I dance I feel like I'm transported to another place. I also benefit from sitting still or lying as if I'm on the beach absorbing sun. For you it could be meditating or taking long walks. What things prevent you from feeling great about each day? What things can you take action toward removing or eliminating in your life? Figure out what you need to incorporate into and or remove from your life in order to truly enjoy each day.

In addition to adding things that provide you pleasure and removing things that do not, you can also be extremely present in every moment that you have. I attended college in Philadelphia and after moving back home to Chicago I continued to visit my best friend who lived there for many years after graduation. During one visit, as we were driving I admired the leaves on the trees that were changing colors before they would all soon fall. How is it that I never noticed the leaves changing colors? How much beauty surrounds us all the time that we don't even notice or appreciate? Open your eyes to the beauty around you every day and recognize how amazing life really is. Until the next time you can schedule a "vacation," there are wonders to witness right in your backyard.

Day 9 – Happiness Takeaways:

1. Incorporate vacation into your daily life.
2. You should have the time of your life every day.
3. Open your eyes to see the beauty around you.
4. If you look for light and beauty you will find it.

Reflection Questions

- What simple activities make you happy?
- Do you do them enough?
- Can you sacrifice something that makes you unhappy to make time to do something that makes you ridiculously happy?
- How can you incorporate more things that make you happy in between the daily activities that you have to do, that don't make you happy?
- How can you capture memories from happy times?
- Can you add tangible objects that elicit good memories, into your work space?

DAY 10

Plant Good Seeds.

**"Everything that exists is in a manner the seed
of that which will be." – Marcus Aurelius**

Sowing and reaping are not new concepts. They are
commonly referred to in religious doctrine, and they
are known to some as karma. In the natural realm the
reality is manifested with crops; a farmer sows or plants
seeds and she reaps a harvest. In order to have crops to
show for, she must first plant seeds. Just as humility is
essential to strong character, so is understanding sowing and reaping in order to sustain a happy life.

A farmer plants corn seeds in the spring, corn stalks
grow, and in the fall she harvests corn. The same is true
for anything else in life. The law of sowing and reaping
is one that can't be broken. We plant seeds every day
and we also reap the harvest of what we planted. If
you examine the life of a person that receives a lot of
kindness and love, you would undoubtedly find that
person gives an abundance of kindness and love to
others. Those who receive generous gifts are people
that give abundantly.

What is it in your life you are hoping to harvest? Look at your life today and you can easily see what it is you are planting to understand your current harvest. Are people constantly mean and rude to you? Do you often feel mistreated or misunderstood? Examine how you treat people. Are you planting the seeds you want to receive? If you are displeased with your most recent harvest, it is never too late to change the seeds that you are planting.

Someone who invests greatly in their friendships and relationships is not the person who is in the hospital without a single visitor. Someone who laughs a lot and is full of joy, is not the same person who spends their time being negative and focused on the faults of others.

Do farmers plant beans and expect corn? Do they plant squash and expect watermelon to grow? Why do we plant seeds of a certain nature and expect something else to grow in their place? The crops in your field are a result of what you have planted. If you want different crops, then plant different seeds. Take a moment and just be really honest with yourself. Are you really giving that which you want to receive? Are certain things in your life dissatisfactory because you are going through a rough season, or is it simply because you have planted bad seeds, and your harvest reflects what you've planted?

Farmers periodically change the crops they plant in their fields. If you wish to harvest a different crop than you have been receiving, you can modify what you are planting. If you need more money, you can start by giving more to others. If you have issues in relationships, then be a better friend, sibling or partner. If you need to change what you are planting, the opportunity to do so is always available. Instead of looking at how someone else's behavior can change your life, look inside of yourself and be completely honest about what you find. If you need to plant different seeds, start doing so immediately. If you are already planting the right seeds, just wait for your crop to develop and mature.

I remember when my paternal grandmother died. I didn't always understand how great my grandmother was, but before she passed away I was fortunate enough to truly appreciate the extent of her greatness. She was in the hospital for about a week before her transition, and I was so annoyed when I went to visit because I could never have time alone with her. There was always a room full of people and a group in the waiting room. Her funeral was like a celebrity funeral. It was as though a pillar of the community passed away. There were hundreds of people who came to celebrate her life, and each person there had a story of how she had personally impacted their lives. Her life overflowed with love and joy, but it was because of how she lived her life. She was the ultimate planter of good seeds.

Before you make excuses or blame weather conditions on your dissatisfactory harvest, take a step back and examine the seeds that you are planting.

Day 10 – Happiness Takeaways:

1. You get back what you give.
2. If you don't like what you are getting take a look and re-evaluate what you are giving.
3. Don't give just to receive in return.
4. Treat others in the way that you want to be treated.
5. Live your life in a way that you don't have to fear what will come back to you, because bad seeds will return in some way, shape, or form.

Reflection Questions

- What seeds have you planted that yielded a favorable harvest?
- What seeds have you planted that yielded an unfavorable harvest?
- What good seeds have you planted lately?
- In what area of your life can you plant better seeds?
- What area of your life hasn't yielded a harvest?

DAY 11

Just Make it Happen.

**"Well done is better than well
said." – Benjamin Franklin**

When I was a child I wanted to be countless things; a
doctor, a teacher, an astronaut, a flight attendant, and a
financial advisor, among other things. Every time I was
exposed to a new career, that's generally what I wanted
to grow up to become. I remember one "career day"
in elementary school, a flight attendant spoke to my
class. I was so intrigued by the idea of travelling all of
the time. She told us that you could even take classes to
learn how to fly airplanes. For the next week my goal in
life was to become a flight attendant that would eventually transition to piloting.

Then, when I was in sixth grade, I won a writing
contest called "Young Authors." I have always had a
knack for writing, but I didn't realize I was a talented
writer until college. Over time, people who came across
my writing gave really good feedback, and at some point
in my early 20's I finally recognized my own talent. I
imagined myself as a writer, and I knew that it was part

of my purpose to share my thoughts and ideas with the world through written word. I spoke of it constantly. "I'm going to be a writer," I would say, or "When I'm a writer," I would mention. For a few years this conversation with me and others regarding my writing continued. I would try to come up with a few pages here and there, yet there was no dedication or discipline. I sincerely believed with everything within me that I was destined to be published, but I guess somewhere in the mix, I lost sight of actually putting in the work.

Eventually I got it; I bought a notebook and I wrote like crazy. I still write constantly. One day I made my typical "When I'm a writer" comment and I annoyed myself to the point of rolling my eyes. Do you really believe in your dream? Do you believe that you can realize your dream? Why are you still talking about it and not actually putting it into action?

Every now and then I encounter someone who complains about "working for the man." I had a friend once say that it's a dumb idea to put your intelligence toward making money for someone else. "Why would a smart person spend his time making someone else rich?" they would ask. More often than not I hear this sort of grumbling from people who are working for someone else; people who aren't entrepreneurs. Visionaries don't have to tell everyone that it's dumb to work for the man. They start their own companies. They don't talk about pursuing their passions, they just do it.

When you're a child, it makes sense to consider what you will become when you grow up. When you're an adult still talking about what you will do when you grow up, you are less likely to make things happen. Put very simply, the older you get, you have less time to actually make your dreams come true. That doesn't mean they can't come true, but spending the years talking about your dreams and not actually acting on them, just doesn't make sense.

What were you planning to become that you have yet to make happen, but you still talk about and dream of? Perhaps it is your destiny to become what it is that you were talking about; maybe that actually is your purpose in life. But it will never happen until you put it into action. It's not too late to go back to school, or to learn a new skill, or to travel, or to do whatever it is that you keep talking about. Stop talking and take action. More action and less conversation will lead you where you want to go.

This concept goes far beyond careers and business goals. There are lots of things we talk about that some of us actually never do. If you have said recently that you are going to actually lose weight, actually start exercising, actually start remodeling your kitchen, actually take a trip, actually open your heart to another person, actually reach out to an old friend, or actually fill in the blank, today please stop talking about it. Don't ever mention it again. Do not verbalize one more time what it is that you are actually planning to do.

Just do it! Begin the work right now. Make it happen. You don't have to talk about it. You don't have to call your friends first and ask their opinions. You don't have to re-arrange your life to do it. Just do it. Before you can stop yourself, and before you start to doubt, just do it. Don't procrastinate as you have been doing. Just take a stand against yourself; refuse to drag your feet any longer. Shut up, and do it.

Day 11 – Happiness Takeaways:

1. Stop talking about it and just go do it.
2. Figure out what it is that is holding you back and fix it.
3. If you don't have enough knowledge to figure out how to get what you want, get more knowledge.
4. Exert more energy toward doing what you need to do.
5. Taking action toward fulfilling your dreams and goals will make you happier than just talking about them.

Reflection Questions

- Why do you procrastinate?
- What is your game plan for achieving your goal?
- Do you have time in your current life space to do what it takes to reach your goals?
- Do you have an accountability partner?
- Can you imagine your life in the future without reaching that goal?
- How much is your future goal worth to you?

Day 12

Keep it to Yourself.

"Silence is a source of great strength." – Lao Tzu

I'm really social and I always have a lot of associates and friends in my life. I love to connect and share my interests with other people. I enjoy spending time with friends and exchanging stories about our experiences. Though I do my best to include people in my life that are wise and whose advice I trust, I came to a place on my journey where I couldn't reveal everything that I was doing to everyone. As I ventured down the path of understanding my purpose and the importance of living a more fulfilled life, I realized how critical it was to treat my dreams and ideas as sacred things.

This idea was especially tough for me because I talk so much! I get excited about ideas, and before I know it I've shared them with every stranger that passes me by on the street. When I quit my first job, though I knew it was what I wanted and needed to do, I couldn't make the decision without the feedback of other people. During certain relationships I relied on the words of my friends to feel confident about staying in something or walking away. Through the valleys that I have walked through, I couldn't have made it without people who I loved speaking words of hope and encouragement to me.

I thrive on the love and support of my friends and family. Through everything in my life that I attempted or tried, it was important to me to have my mother's approval in particular. But there came a time in my life where I had to walk certain roads alone, and I stopped looking to my mother or anyone for approval. My family and friends were still around, but they couldn't make certain things happen in my life. The advice of my friends wasn't what I needed to cause progress to transpire in my life, and I didn't need their confirmation because I knew deep down inside what would propel me forward. If you have faith, do you need a green light from someone to legitimize what you believe? Confirmation is nice to have from others, but is it always necessary? If you know with everything inside of you that you should pursue something or take action toward a goal, or maybe even walk away from something you're involved in, do you really need to get your friend's advice about it?

When I first started keeping things to myself, my intention was not to keep secrets, but to preserve the innocence of my dreams and to keep them sacred. I believe my friends love me and have my best interest at heart. However, when you expose certain things to people, they feel compelled to speculate, or give their opinion. Sometimes this may cause you to doubt yourself or grow frustrated, and I was so confident in my purpose, so sure of what I heard spoken in my Spirit, that I didn't need confirmation from outside sources.

I knew I couldn't reach my destination and my destiny, solely because of the support of my loved ones; I had to rely on my faith and hard work. Though this may be as challenging for you as it was for me, sometimes you have to refrain from sharing everything with everyone. Your family and friends love you; however, there are things in your life that they won't understand about you and your desires. Their lack of understanding might cause you to doubt or have fear that you can have what you want. Sometimes people won't understand your commitment to your faith, but you can't give up just because someone thinks that you are crazy.

Though your friends love you, there are also times when they may not actually wish for your success. It is possible for your loved ones to envy what you are trying to accomplish. Perhaps they don't want you to leave them behind, or they expect that your success will change you. Regardless, concealing your dreams leaves less opportunity for others to speak ill of what you want to accomplish. You really don't need extra negative energy released toward your goal.

No one wants you to live the life you know you were destined for more than you, well and maybe your mother.

No one wants you to fulfill your purpose more than you. When you want something and believe it is for you, as in its part of your destiny or your purpose, you have to believe in it. Regardless of what your friends or family think. It doesn't matter if other people don't understand your feelings or your commitment to your dream. If you believe, then it will happen. Stop looking for confirmation from others and trust what is in your heart.

Sometimes it is necessary to share your ideas with others as you may need help to make your dream a reality. Perhaps you need investors, or someone who has already done what you want to do to provide insight or mentorship. As John Donne said, "no man is an island entire of itself." No one who is successful achieved their success solely on their own. There were other people involved. My point isn't for you to isolate yourself from others or live in a world where nothing exists besides you and your faith. I simply want to remind you that it is important to treat your dreams, ideas and goals as sacred things, and for you to be confident in trusting yourself.

In times when you find it necessary to confide in loved ones, make sure that you aren't broadcasting things or discussing them casually until you have confidently made certain decisions. Until you are steady and sure, sharing your fragile ideas and thoughts with fewer people is ideal.

Day 12 – Happiness Takeaways:

1. Being silent helps you figure things out and reach conclusions without the opinions of others.
2. Sharing your vision with others can lead to exposing it to negativity and doubt.
3. Don't share your vision and let someone discourage you or cause you to have fear about accomplishing your goal.
4. Don't let a loved one's negativity derail your dream.

Reflection Questions

- Do you believe your goals and dreams are sacred?
- Why do you tell people things before they are solid plans?
- Do you need the encouragement of others to feel secure about your ideas?
- What do you gain from telling casual acquaintances about your goals?
- What do you risk when you don't share your ideas with others?
- Can you make a decision without confirmation from your loved ones?

Day 13

Stop Hating.

"Envy is a waste of time." – Author Unknown

In college I was extremely envious of my high school best friend. I struggled so much academically and sometimes socially, and I had countless challenges, while her life just seemed too easy. She was thriving and I thought I was slowly disintegrating. I was very unhappy, and I kept thinking that her life was so much better than mine. College was a time in my life where I envied a lot. There were a lot of wealthy students at the school I attended, and I used to think that if I grew up wealthier my experiences and my life would have been better.

The reality is that it was easier for me to look at other's lives and make judgments about what they had that I didn't have, instead of improving myself. The reason for most of my challenges then was simply because of me. It didn't occur to me at the time to address my imperfections and character flaws. I wasted so much time focusing my energy on being resentful and envious of others; precious time that I could have spent in more productive ways, like studying.

At some point, my envy began to impact my relationships. I was so jealous of some of the people who I cared about that I couldn't enjoy time spent with them. Instead of being happy for my friends, I was jealous. I became annoyed with myself because envy takes a lot of energy and I realized that if I continued along the same path, I wouldn't have any friends at all. I loved my friends and I didn't want to lose my relationships, so I had to make a conscious decision to eliminate jealous thoughts as they came to me. Over time, I became really good at managing my jealous emotions. I can honestly say that today, I am genuinely happy for my friends' successes.

Getting past my jealousy took two main steps. First, I had to spend time accepting accountability for my life; my actions led to my situation, and that my current predicament was no one's fault but my own. If things weren't working out for me, I couldn't take it out on someone else. While it is easier to move the spotlight to someone else and minimize what they are doing with their life, it is not healthy and it causes you to stay in the same envious place. You can't be jealous of others and happy with your life at the same time.

Secondly, I had to accept that the world didn't revolve around me. Why would the success of someone else immediately cause me to think about myself and how their success made me feel? How silly is that? Why should someone else's life and how they live it make me feel insecure? You should be able to think of someone else in a positive way without considering yourself and how their life makes you feel. Life isn't all about you or me.

Today I can celebrate the success of my friends and the light in their lives. I take ownership for my life and my decisions and I realize that my success or lack of it is because of me and my decisions. Life is not a competition, and supporting my loved ones and believing for them makes me happier than being jealous or envious of them. When others succeed, it encourages me that I can reach my goals as well.

It amazes me how frequently people direct negative energy toward someone just because they are jealous. It is all too common that someone has something bad to say about the prettiest girl in the room. Does it impact your life that she is pretty? Do you feel better after speaking negatively about her or wishing you looked as good? Do you feel more important by saying that the rich guy at the party that everyone is talking about is probably stupid? Or saying that if he didn't have a trust fund to fall back on he wouldn't be so successful? You are wasting energy.

Learn to admire instead of envy. Appreciate the most attractive person in the room. Learn from the guy that makes great business decisions. Instead of minimizing others so that you can feel better about yourself, become a better person by taking notice of the success of others. Learn to be happy for other people. If you can be happy for someone else, you can believe that something good will happen in your own life.

Envy is like poison to our dreams. It distracts us from our own goal and mission. "If only I had what she had, I would be able to reach my goal. If only I went to school where he did, I would be so much further ahead." Isn't it easier to say those things than to take responsibility for your own progress, or lack thereof? The reality is that even if you had the thing someone else has, that you are convinced makes all the difference, you would find some other excuse as to why you haven't achieved your dream.

Stop looking around at everyone else. Who cares what everyone else is doing? Their behaviors and or activities are not going to advance you. If you direct your focus toward what you need to accomplish, you might actually get somewhere. Envy takes a lot of energy. Letting it go will free up a lot of thought space and drive; you'll be surprised what you can do when you set it aside. As long as you are planting envious seeds, you will never become secure and confident in yourself and your abilities.

Day 13 – Happiness Takeaways:

1. Life isn't a competition against other people.
2. Stop comparing yourself to others.
3. Don't hate on someone that is doing something better and bigger than you.
4. Admire without envy.
5. Take sincere pleasure in the success of your friends and loved ones.
6. Be inspired by the success of other people.
7. Jealous people are not happy with their own lives.

Reflection Questions

- How do you feel when someone has something that you want but that you don't have?
- Do you compare yourself to other people? Why?
- What makes you jealous?
- Is it hard for you to be happy for others?
- Do you feel better about yourself when you speak negatively about someone else?

DAY 14

Learn When to Leave the Party.

"Everyone has that friend that doesn't get the hint when it's time to go home." - Unknown

When I was in my early 20s I went out faithfully every weekend. I got dressed up, often wearing uncomfortable outfits and shoes, put a lot of effort into my hair and make-up (which always looked amazing), and ventured out to the parties advertised as being "the place to be." My friends and I would stand in lines at the "hottest party," sometimes even in the cold, hoping to have the time of our lives at "the place to be." After spending too much time in line, the actual party rarely lived up to our expectations. However, because going out every weekend is what young 20 year olds do, we would stay out really late, usually because we put so much effort into our going out preparation. I couldn't leave the party immediately because I felt as though all of my effort to get ready would be a waste of time.

I have a lot of wonderful memories from going out with friends from those days. However, as I got older I changed my approach to going out. I started spending my time doing things that I loved without regard to how cool or how sought-out the party that I would attend was expected to be. One night I went out to dinner at a Latin restaurant, and fell in love with salsa dancing. For three years of my life, my behavior was dictated by my love for salsa dancing. I would wear clothing that was comfortable to dance in, and I wouldn't wear a lot of make-up because it never lasted beyond my second dance of the night. One day years later I woke up and realized that salsa was no longer "it" for me, and I began to seek my enjoyment elsewhere.

As an experienced "partier" I've learned how important it is to know when to leave the party. There have been times when I wore my favorite dress, had my hair specially styled, stood in line for an hour, and had a horrible time at a party. Sometimes in life it is important to assess a situation, realize that it's not what you expected, and find solace in walking away. There are times when we know something is not going to get better, but we've invested so much in it, so we trudge on, not really expecting things to improve, yet feeling badly for walking away because of the time we have already spent. Investing more time in a sinking ship, is consciously deciding to keep wasting your time. At the point where you are confident your ship can't be saved, it is okay to move on. What is to be said of your invested time once the ship sinks and you go down with it? Nothing. You can't recover your time; however, you can stop spending your time unwisely once you understand the party you are at is not going to get better.

Perhaps you have an old, dear friend who has proven they don't have the character you thought. Should you remain friends with them because you've known them forever, even though it is evident that nothing positive will ever result from knowing that person? Or maybe you went to school for a career and you expected it would provide fulfillment, but after years of actually working in it, you feel like part of your soul has died. However, you feel like you can't walk away or reconsider a new career path because of the time you spent in school. Of course, you don't want to feel like all of your time was wasted. But can't you actually just walk away right now? Is it better to stay in something just because walking away will make you feel as though you wasted your time? Isn't staying a choice to continue to waste your time? Which is the lesser of two evils: continuing to waste time knowingly or walking away and saving the time you have moving forward? Maybe you don't want to walk away because you don't want to "quit." It's better to quit when something isn't working and try something else than to keep doing something that isn't working.

Of course I've also been to parties where I had a great time, and chose to leave before the party ended. "Ang this is such a great time, why are you leaving?" Sometimes you should leave the party on a high note. If I sought to have an amazing time and I achieved that goal, then I am pretty comfortable leaving a party. I consider this concept similarly to the idea of not overstaying your welcome. My family has had many parties that have gone well, and there is always that person who just won't go home. That person that misses the "party is over" message always leaves a bad taste in your mouth.

If you are seeking something in your life and you receive it, you might feel compelled to continue a connection that doesn't need to be continued. Have you had friends who you've really liked and then something happened and you fell out of touch? You say to yourself all the time, "Oh yes I remember that person. We had some great times. I'm going to call him one of these days." Why? If you still haven't done it, you probably won't and that is okay. You left the party on a high note. Enjoy the memories and move on. It is okay to leave a party while you are still enjoying yourself. Maybe things are going amazingly at work, but you feel deep inside that your purpose lies elsewhere. Just because things are going well doesn't mean you need to stay. Don't be afraid to pursue something else because you fear that things can't get any better. If your Spirit is leading you elsewhere, chances are, there is something better.

Finally, there is the scenario where you are at a party, and at some point the outcome seems uncertain. Maybe your friends showed up late or the cost to enter was more than you expected. Perhaps the DJ was terrible and just as you were on your way out to leave, your favorite DJ took the platform. You hoped to have an amazing time, and while you didn't see clear evidence that you would, you didn't stop believing and you ended up at the party that actually turned out to be the time of your life. Perhaps you knew in your Spirit that you were where you were supposed to be. You heard from your inner voice very clearly and every cell in your body believed to the point of knowing that you were at the right party.

Yet, circumstances didn't appear so.

The week before my 28th birthday, I endured a horrible break up. My best friend Nicole flew into town at the last minute and I made plans for us to go dancing at an outdoor festival with several other friends. I clearly remember the weather for that day had rain in the forecast and I kept saying "I don't care if it is supposed to rain, I'm not changing my plans." We went dancing and I had the time of my life. I danced until my clothes were soaked with sweat. That day is one of my best memories.

The rain didn't arrive until after the dance festival ended. It's almost as if God held the rain until my celebration was over. I knew I was supposed to be there and no circumstance could convince me otherwise. Maybe you are having a rough time in your marriage, or maybe you are struggling at a job that you are sure holds purpose to your destiny. If you are where you know you are supposed to be, and if you believe that party will be the time of your life, it will be. Don't be discouraged or distracted by circumstances.

In the party of life, you must know when to leave and when to stay. Whether you should leave early, leave while the party is going strong, or stay until the end, trust your instincts and have a good time.

Day 14 – Happiness Takeaways:

1. If walking away is the best thing to do, do it.
2. If you can't figure out why you are at the party, then it is probably time to leave.
3. Leave or stay at the party because of what you want, not because of what someone else wants.
4. Trust your instincts and learn to rely on them.
5. Making the decision whether to stay or go gets easier over time if you learn to listen to your inner voice.

Reflection Questions

- What is the determining factor as to whether you pursue something, pause, or retreat?
- What is your gut saying about your situation?
- What will you gain and lose if you stay at the party?
- What will you gain and lose if you leave the party?

DAY 15

Ask, Fight, and Take.

**"Is it a crime, to fight, for what
is mine?" – Tupac Shakur**

It took me the majority of my twenties to understand
that no one was going to give me anything when it
came to my career. I have a lot of wonderful qualities
that I am proud of, including my intelligence, persistence, diligence, and most importantly, my humility.
Though I am no shrinking violet, as I live my life with
the mantra "more is more," I greatly admire humility. I've always believed that you should let your light
shine brightly and that others would notice. It never
occurred to me to go around telling people how bright
my light was; I figured if it was shining brightly enough
the right people would notice.

However, I had to finally recognize the fact that in
business the people who advance are not necessarily
the people who perform the best, but the people who
can convince others that their performance is the best.
I often felt like the people who put on the best show
were recognized. Once you add lights, smoke, and

pyrotechnics, a performance appears to be so much more than it really is.

When I worked at my first job out of college, I did my work well, and I was really nice and friendly. I thought that promotion came from being a good employee and from being well liked by everyone. Promotion never came, but I didn't mind because I didn't really enjoy my work at that company, and I really wanted to do something else with my life. I took another job, and another, and another, and I finally realized that people don't get what they want in life by waiting for someone to recognize that they deserve it.

I'm not implying that the humble and deserving are not rewarded in life or in Corporate America, but I am pretty sure that I am not the only one out there that has witnessed people get promoted time and time again; people whose peers in the office would find them undeserving. In my own career I would not change my behavior in the sense of highlighting my own work by hurting someone else, or by rising to the top by stroking the egos of the leadership around me. However, I would be more vocal regarding my own accomplishments and successes, making sure that leadership understood them. I often relied on my direct bosses to sing my praises, when in reality I should have taken risks and sang my own praises to the people who mattered in terms of bringing about promotion or advancement.

In a job interview you have to convince someone who doesn't know you how great and wonderful you are in order to land the job. This convincing should not stop once you gain the position. As you prove yourself and as your light shines, make sure that the right people take notice. People get what they want in life by promoting themselves. They decide what they want and they take action to get it. If it's a promotion, they do things that say "look at me, I deserve a promotion." They don't wait around to be noticed. They make the person handing out promotions notice them. They will work tirelessly until the right person notices their efforts, and they are willing to speak on their behalf and ask for what they want.

This is true beyond careers and work. In any situation you are dealing with, faith is essential, but faith alone is not enough. In addition to faith and hard work, you have to align yourself with key decision makers as well as be willing to ask for what you want. I've never thought it was fair for people who are often less deserving to get ahead in life, however, I couldn't be angry with anyone but myself for my lack of promotion, until I became more vocal and asked for what I wanted.

You can't just sit around expecting anyone to hand you what it is that you want in a neat little package. If that's how you get what you want out of life, good for you; however, if it's not, don't be uncomfortable with asking, or even fighting for or taking what you want. I know quite a few smart people who are nice and have done and said all of the right things, yet they haven't advanced to where they want to be. What separates them from those who do get to where they want to be is the willingness to ask, fight, and take.

We were created with everything we need to transport our dreams from our imaginations into reality. We already have what it takes to make things happen for our lives inside of us. Any lack of resources that we have, He has given us the ability to retrieve that which we need. He has also given us the ability to believe that divine connections and doors of opportunity will be opened. Though we have to expect the universe to conspire for our well beings, we also have to work hard, and ask, fight, and take, in order to reach our goals.

As long as you sit around waiting for the sky to open up and deposit your dream or goal to you from heaven, it isn't going to happen. You already have what you need. When you make it happen it will happen. No one is going to do it for you. No one is going to work harder for your dream than you. No one is going to believe harder for your goals than you. No one is going to make something happen for you better than you can. Maybe you can't make it happen in a matter of minutes. But you can make it happen. You have to, because if you don't, it's not going to happen. Ask, fight, and take.

Make it happen!

Day 15 – Happiness Takeaways:

1. You have to take what you want.
2. You are less likely to receive if you never ask.
3. Promoting yourself doesn't make you arrogant.
4. Maintaining confidence and humility at the same time is possible.
5. Share your accomplishments with others.

Reflection Questions

- Are you good at self-promotion?
- Are you embarrassed to tell others about your strengths and accomplishments?
- If so, why?
- Is self-promotion at odds with humility?
- If you don't tell people certain things about yourself how will they know?
- Does your boss know all of your strengths, interests, and goals as they relate to your professional career at your current job?
- How does it make you feel when others around you who are less qualified become promoted?

DAY 16

Trust the Process.

**"Don't be discouraged. It's often
the last key in the bunch that opens
the lock." – Author Unknown**

I'm a believer. I believe that God loves me, and that the universe conspires in my favor. I believe that when things don't go well for me at the moment, there is still something to be gained. I believe that when my plans don't work out the way I expected, God has something different in mind than I did. I believe there is a bigger picture and though I have not fit all of the pieces together, the pieces already exist and will fit into place in God's timing. I don't just say these things; I really do believe them deep down in my heart.

We are all coming from a different place and point of view, but you likely have established the set of values and principles that you support and believe. Maybe you aren't a Christian like me, but I wanted you to understand my point of view. I have experienced a lot and reacted differently than some people because of faith. Sometimes I wonder if the people around me think I'm crazy for not being negative or fearful during certain times in my life, but I genuinely don't worry about a lot of things that other people commonly do. I sincerely believe that though I can't see the big picture, I know that there is one. Everything happens for a reason, even if you don't know what it is.

Despite my full belief that things will work out for me, I am still human and not divine. As strong as my faith is, there are times in my life when the voices of fear and doubt are so loud that I can't ignore them:

> "If things were going to work out, wouldn't they have worked out by now?"

> "You're lying to yourself Angela."

> "You aren't good enough for what it is that you want out of life."

> "The things that you are expecting to happen, don't work out for people like you."

The voices of fear and doubt are very powerful and they are cruel and unkind. Circumstances have come that caused me to doubt. I actively work to eliminate thoughts of doubt because my faith can't thrive in the presence of it. I will never forget sitting on my couch one day watching the episode preceding the season finale of a popular weight loss show. There was a contestant who worked really hard to be a finalist, and he was one episode away from the finals. He was in third place and the only contestants guaranteed a spot in the finals were in first and second place. The competition was opened up to other contestants that already left the show, and he had to compete against all of them in order to qualify for the last opening in the finals, which he had not expected.

He grew extremely frustrated with the uncertainty of his fate, and instead of fueling his determination his anger distracted his focus from his workouts. One of the trainers was so in sync with him that he sensed the change in his drive, and his shifting energy. The trainer approached him and asked him why he was distracted. The contestant explained his disappointment over having to compete against multiple competitors to make it as a finalist. He had come so close, and then the finals were suddenly snatched out of his reach. What seemed like a realistic goal had suddenly turned into a goal that he would never achieve.

The trainer got in his face, looked into his eyes and yelled "Trust the process!" At the moment the trainer spoke to the contestant, it was as if the trainer was speaking to me. "Trust the process, trust the process, trust the process." I began to dwell on those three words. If everything I initially said about my faith or what I believe is true, then I need to trust the process.

It's easy to believe that things will work out for you when everything is already working out. It is not far-fetched to say that the sun will shine, when the sun is actually shining. But when lightning, thunder and rain are more evident and constant than the sun, it's easy to believe that there is no sun. If rainy Monday turned into a season of rain that never ended, you might stop believing that the sun would ever shine again.

I was driving to work one day and witnessed the most beautiful sight in the sky of the sun peeking through the clouds in a very gloomy sky. The sun is always shining. Though we can't always see it, the fact remains that the sun continues to emit energy and light. When it is night where I am, it is day time someplace else. There isn't a moment when the sun is not shining, whether I can see it or not. If a dark cloud surrounded the earth today, the sun would still be shining in the center of our universe.

There is more to life than what you are experiencing right now. Even creation did not happen in a day. It was a process. If you don't share my faith and you believe in evolution, that too was a process. As long as the sun shines, you can trust that there is a process. Don't let rejection or disappointment distract you from your goal. The contestant went on to win the competition. All he had to do was trust the process.

Day 16 – Happiness Takeaways:

1. There is a bigger picture.
2. The universe conspires for your success.
3. Things will fall into place.
4. The sun is always shining.
5. When the process is at its toughest, trust more.

Reflection Questions

- Do you ever struggle to find the light?
- How do you overcome darkness in your life?
- What process do you need to trust in right now?
- Do challenges discourage you or motivate you?
- How can you overcome your current challenges?

DAY 17

Get Comfortable with Sacrifice.

"I think the good and the great are only separated by the willingness to sacrifice." – Kareem Abdul-Jabbar

I remember when I started blogging. One of my friends had an event website and she asked me to blog for her site which I did nearly every week for almost two years. I loved sharing my thoughts and my heart with others. I've always been a writer, and finally I became tired of listening to myself say that I wanted to write. Writing is such an easy thing to do; there are no barriers to entry, and there is no special education required. You don't even need technology, as you can still write the old fashioned way if necessary. If you want to write, you write; it really is just that simple.

I learned a lot about sacrifice from a really good friend of mine. Bri went back to school to pursue a master's degree in nursing. Her story is a great one. She went to college determined to be an engineer. After five years she received her degree, and soon after decided that she didn't actually want to be an engineer. She worked for an industrial distributor doing international sales and customer service, for several years before deciding to pursue nursing. Once she decided that she wanted to be a nurse, she went back to school without a second thought. I admire my friend for committing so easily to her goal; but I digress.

Bri had a lot of schoolwork because her program was full time, and she didn't have an abundance of time since she was still working 30 hours a week. As she didn't have a lot of extra time for social engagements, we would use our time spent together for her to study and for me to write. Initially I would surf the web and entertain myself in multiple ways besides writing. I did the majority of my writing when she and I would meet, which would amount to an hour or two a week or so on average.

I couldn't spend as much time writing as I wanted to because I had a very full social calendar. I loved sharing meals with friends, and as I had always made time to spend with my friends during the week, I didn't think twice about making plans. Before I knew it I had planned something to do every night, leaving no time for writing, and this continued to happen week after week.

One day I was talking to Bri and she told me that I would never finish my book until I truly committed to it. I thought about it, and I realized she was right, but I couldn't figure out how to incorporate writing into my schedule that was already full. The same week she said that to me, I attended an event through work, where the speaker who was a famous pastor said that it is not easy giving birth to our dreams. Until we truly commit to them, they won't happen. Making our dreams and goals become a reality takes a lot of hard work and sacrifice.

It took me some time to give up some of my social activity in order for my writing to live. I always felt that after an eight to ten hour workday that I deserved to take a break and hang out with my friends. While I couldn't create more time in my day, I started managing my time in a way that my writing took precedence over my socialization. I soon found that sacrificing my social activities led me to do something daily that actually fulfilled me. I would write after work and feel more like myself than I ever had. The more I wrote the more I understood why it was meaningful for me to sacrifice my social agenda. I gained so much that I stopped feeling like I was actually losing anything.

The more I gave up what I thought I needed, the more I opened myself to other things that actually were fulfilling. As self-aware as I've always thought I was, I learned a lot about myself when I spent more time writing alone, than talking and spending time with other people. Life is full of seasons. I didn't plan to always remain less social, but it was necessary at the time. Until I was willing to sacrifice I wasn't able to reach my goal.

Reaching my goal required me to sacrifice my time, but for you it might require something else. Your goal might require a sacrifice that is financial, physical, or something else altogether. Regardless what it is that you need to sacrifice it is safe to say that until you commit enough to your dream to sacrifice something, it probably won't happen. If it means enough to you, give up what you need to in order to progress. Your sacrifice isn't necessarily one that will endure forever, but for now, you have to become comfortable with it. If you sacrifice today, you will be happier in the long run.

Day 17 – Happiness Takeaways:

1. Without sacrifice, you won't reach your goal.
2. If it was possible without sacrifice, you would have done it ten times by now.
3. If you don't want it enough to make the sacrifice, then you don't want it enough.
4. Sacrificing today will benefit you in the long run.

Reflection Questions

- Are you willing to give up certain things in order to reach your goals?
- What do you need to sacrifice?
- What aren't you willing to sacrifice?
- What things can you sacrifice today with little regard?

DAY 18

Select your Inner Circle
Carefully.

**"Friendship is one mind in
two bodies." - Mencius**

Who are your friends? Who is in your life? Do they tell you the truth or do they just tell you what you want to hear? Do they tell you when you're wrong, or do they observe silently as you walk down a path that isn't good for you? Do they support you, or do they make you feel badly about trying to reach your goals? Do they encourage you? What do they say about you when you aren't around?

My life has been so rich, so full of love, so wonderful. Life has not been perfect as I've faced as much disappointment and rejection as the next person, maybe even more. I've faced challenges, experienced regret, and I've let myself down. I've made bad decisions, and other good ones that still didn't result in smiles and sunshine. Despite all of the negativity that I've experienced, my life has yielded so much love. I was given a tremendous amount of love as a child, and just as I received an abundance of love then, I give so much today. I was blessed to have a great family, but as I understood the importance of strong relationships, I selected amazing people to enhance the quality of my journey in life.

I have a reputation among my friends for being very selective when it comes to friendships. I actually joked with one of my good friends about being uncertain as to whether I would make a permanent place in my life for her when I first met her. Though I joke about it, there was a time when I wasn't sure. Thankfully I did, because she is a dear friend. Whenever one of my friends says "oh you have to meet so and so, you will love her," I'm immediately skeptical because I don't just invite everyone into my life.

Having good friends alone is not enough to make or break your happiness, but they are a critical component for sure. I think of friends as the cheerleaders or pep squad of a sports team. Your friends are the people who change your bike tires and hand you a fresh water bottle when you are doing a race. Friends are the team of people who do your hair and makeup and make sure your outfit is perfect before the camera starts rolling. If you have great friends, you can only become a better person.

I am friendly and I will spend time with practically anyone. I have countless relationships from different jobs that I've worked, church, school, and from years going out dancing. Though I know a lot of people, only a small group composes my inner circle. My inner circle has people who really understand me and can be trusted with my heart. It is my job to guard my heart, and as I love deeply, it is my obligation to protect my heart from people until I know that they can be trusted. Before you allow someone into the sacred place of your inner circle you have to know that they will not abuse the responsibility.

I never had a sister, but I truly believe that my friends are just as great as sisters ever could be for me. They really are my soul mates. Though we don't always agree, they are on my team and they really desire my success. They are also willing to tell me when I am wrong. One of my friends and I grew disconnected because I was holding a grudge over something petty, and eventually though I got over it, we didn't really resume constant contact. Despite our distance, I could still rely on her to be present in my life when it mattered, and as I would expect her to, she did. Even when we weren't physically connected, I could still trust her to support me and be there for me, as I was for her.

We all need people to join us along our journeys. I believe it is important to generally be social and friendly with all people. However, I strongly warn anyone to take friendships very seriously and enter them with caution. Just as you would evaluate someone to determine if you wanted to date them, the same should be done with the friends that we allow in our inner circles. There is power in having an exceptional team of people on your side, so make sure that you are kindred spirits and of the same mind before you reveal your heart and consider someone a true friend. Take inventory of your relationships and make sure that the people in your life are in the positions that they should be.

Day 18 – Happiness Takeaways:

1. You need to be selective with who you allow in your life.
2. If you can't define purpose in a relationship, end the relationship.
3. If you want great friends, be a great friend.
4. Take care of your relationships. Invest in them, nourish them, and participate in them.
5. Be cautious and careful when allowing people to speak into your life.

Reflection Questions

- Who are the five most influential people in your life?
- What do you admire and respect about each person?
- How does each person contribute to your success?
- How do you contribute to their success?
- Can you define purpose in all of your relationships?
- How can you be a better friend to those in your inner circle?

DAY 19

Speak Life.

**"Death and life are in the power of
the tongue." – Proverbs 18:21**

Words are not simply sounds uttered through the lips.
Words are so much more. The Bible states that death
and life are in the power of the tongue; they can kill
or give life. Words can tear down or they can build up.

There are several famous sayings expressing the
power of words, one of them being the following:

> "You can say anything to someone; it's just a
> matter of how you say it."

I believe there is some merit to this. However,
before we speak at all, we should critically evaluate the
impact or consequences of our words. Some things
must be said, so it's true that we should be strategic in
the words we select.

> "Sticks and stones may break my bones but
> words never hurt me."

If only that one was true. What joke or comment did someone make that hurt your feelings and has stuck with you your entire life? Maybe you have moved past the pain it caused, and those same words have lost their power to hurt you. But isn't it true that you still remember? Perhaps you aren't hurting today, but you can still remember the pain. There are a lot of wounded people, struggling to overcome harmful words that were spoken to them in their pasts and in their present.

Some things are simply better left unsaid. If the words you speak bring more death than life, why are you saying them? I realize there are times when things in our lives need to be torn down or broken, but make sure your words aren't being spoken simply to hurt people because as you know for yourself those memories can't be removed. Don't speak anything to someone that you wouldn't like having spoken to you.

I used to make a statement regularly about one of my friends, and to me it didn't seem like I was saying anything hurtful. "Even if I decided to stop being your friend my family would still invite you to our parties!" Our friendship was stronger than ever, and in my mind my comment simply conveyed how good of friends we were. It turns out that my comment insulted my friend and one day she asked me why I kept saying it. I apologized and I stopped making the comment because it was important to me not to offend my friend. While I thought I was making a harmless joke, she took my comment as so much more.

As powerful as words are, they are not tangible. Once spoken, they can't be physically removed from the atmosphere. Once they land on an ear, the impact is realized. Words are so powerful that they can be used to move you toward your dreams or to bring death to your dream. Do your words support your vision? "That will never happen for me" or "I don't think I can" or "nothing ever works out for me" are words you should never speak. If you believe, if you truly have faith, your words will reflect your faith.

If you are ever going to realize your dreams you have to do more than work toward them. You have to breathe life into them. Words are life; therefore you must use words to bring your vision to life. If you want to be happy, you have to speak against the things in your life that are unhappy. Use words as a tool to reach your goals in life.

"I will reach my dreams."

"I will have an amazing day."

"I believe."

"My dream will become my reality."

"My relationships are strong and healthy."

"I live a healthy lifestyle."

"My light shines brightly and impacts the world."

"I can achieve anything."

"I will overcome my challenges."

"The possibilities for my life are endless."

"I attract positivity."

"Challenges make me stronger, and get me closer to my destination."

"I am a winner!"

Day 19 – Happiness Takeaways:

1. Speak of things that you want to happen as if they are going to happen.
2. Be confident you will reach your goals and dreams.
3. Don't allow doubt and fear to extend beyond your thoughts.
4. Don't convert negative thoughts to words.
5. Don't speak negatively about others.
6. Don't be a verbal dream killer.

Reflection Questions

- Are your words about your life and others' more often positive or negative?
- Do you jokingly say negative or destructive statements?
  - What are they?
  - Why do you say them?
- Do you positively affirm yourself verbally?
- What is your daily affirmation that encourages you?

DAY 20

Eliminate Life-Limiting Thoughts.

"As a man thinketh, so is he." – Proverbs 23:7

I remember as a child my classmates expressing things like wanting to be President or an astronaut. I recall thinking "wow that's unlikely." I always thought that you had to be "special" to accomplish such careers, but who determines what "special" is? Though I had quite the imagination as a child, my restrictive thoughts led me to believe that I was destined to live a life built upon limitations. I can't quite pinpoint where those thoughts came from, as my parents never planted the idea that there was anything that I couldn't do or be.

We are all special and though everyone can't be President of the United States given the limited number of openings, we all have unique talents and abilities. We can all achieve significant goals and impact the lives of others. Regardless of the origin of our life-limiting thoughts, we have to start believing that the only limitations that exist in life are things that we give power to. You control what has power in your life through your thoughts. Nothing can prevent you from accomplishing something unless you acknowledge it as having the power to stop you. Your thoughts are the key to whether you choose to live a life with limits or a life beyond limits. If you eliminate your restrictive thoughts, you can live a life beyond limitations.

There are things in life that we never accomplished because someone told us we couldn't and we believed them. Other things we didn't accomplish because we never saw anyone else set the example, or the few examples we had failed in trying to reach certain goals, leaving us with the idea that certain things were impossible. Perhaps you didn't pursue a particular dream because a family member discouraged you. I clearly remember being a girl in the kitchen of my aunt's home with her husband and my brother. My aunt's husband asked my brother what he planned to study in college. My brother said he wanted to be an engineer. My aunt's husband proceeded to tell my brother that it would be very difficult and it was unlikely that he would reach his goal. This negativity was from a guy who didn't even know my brother and his abilities. I asked myself "Who is this guy to tell my brother what he can't be?"

Over time, seeds of discouragement and limitation take root in our hearts and souls. There are many people who model their lives upon fear and limitation and so readily plant these seeds in the mind of others. Once you acknowledge the areas of your life that have not flourished because of your own limiting ideas, it is your responsibility to live in a way that doesn't give those thoughts power. We cannot give our power over to the fears of failure, disappointment, lack, or anything else. Limiting thoughts limit our happiness.

Maybe you want to live abroad for a few years. Or perhaps you don't want to have a traditional life. Maybe you would rather pursue a less lucrative career than what your parents wanted or expected for you. Maybe you didn't pursue higher education because someone led you to believe you weren't smart enough. How many "maybes" exist in your mind because of life-limiting thoughts? It is never too late to pursue the thoughts and dreams that have existed in your soul that until now were overcome by limitation. The limits that have defeated you in the past are not real. They don't exist if you don't give them power.

I was riding the bus one day, reading my Bible when a fellow passenger asked me what church I went to. We had a conversation, though it was largely one sided. He told me about his life and his struggles. He then proceeded to tell me how special and blessed I was, and how amazing my future would be. He was so sure about it, as if he actually knew me and my potential in life. When he got off of the bus, I felt sad because I couldn't figure out how to transfer his thoughts about me to his own life. Here was a stranger, certain of my greatness, that couldn't see his own potential, and who had more hope for my future than his own.

We are all special, and we can all realize greatness in our lives. Getting past the millions of doubts and limiting thoughts that have seeped into our lives is possible. If someone else can do it, why can't you? If someone else has yet to do it, why can't you be the first?

The differentiating factor that separates people living their dreams from people living a life they don't want to live is belief. Believing you can and will do something is the first step to overcome life-limiting thoughts. If you believe you can, you will. If that belief becomes your truth, nothing can separate you from what you want. If you believe you are a person of value, love and light, then you will live your life accordingly. If you believe you are not impactful to the earth and you have no purpose, then your life will be meaningless.

In addition to really believing you can reach your goals, you have to speak against limiting thoughts. Instead of internalizing fear and doubt, whether it developed inside of you or through the words of someone else, reject them. You don't have to consider whether the fear or doubt is merited, because it is not. If you willingly give fear or doubt any power, you will never live beyond limitations.

When you are faced with a limiting thought, consider how accepting the limitation will impact the outcome of your life. Can you accept living a limited life? Imagine how your life could advance if you didn't subscribe to limitations, and internalize that thought. What if you had the chance of a lifetime and you didn't pursue it because you didn't believe you were worthy of the opportunity? Could you live the rest of your life happy knowing you chose to walk away from something great? Could you accept that your life didn't fulfill purpose because of your own fears? Replace the thoughts of you not reaching your goals with thoughts of you thriving and excelling.

Everyone has life-limiting thoughts, obstacles, and challenges that they have to work to overcome. Giving in to thoughts of fear and doubt is simple and requires no effort, but overcoming is a struggle that has to be taken day by day. When you learn to overcome these thoughts, only then can your life advance to a place where you have no regrets. Take back your power over your thoughts.

Day 20 – Happiness Takeaways:

1. Your thoughts control what direction your life heads.
2. If you don't believe you can do it, then you won't.
3. Speak against your negative thoughts.
4. Replace your bad thoughts with good thoughts.
5. Work at controlling the thoughts that you have.
6. Life limiting thoughts, limit your happiness

Reflection Questions

- What are you convinced you aren't good at or that you should never do or pursue?
- Why do you believe you will fail if you try?
- How often do you think "I can't do that?"
- What have you always wanted to pursue but you didn't out of fear?
- Do you think you are worthy of happiness?
- Do you believe?

DAY 21

Be Kind.

"Be kind whenever possible. It is always possible." – Tenzin Gyatso

Kindness encompasses many things. To be kind is to be good, thoughtful, charitable, sympathetic, and gentle, just to name a few. We have many opportunities every day to be kind. We encounter people all of the time that could use a bit of kindness. I love people, and I love knowing that I can impact someone in a big way with even a small gesture. Being kind makes me happy; it offers such a great feeling. The feeling that you receive obviously isn't a reason to be kind, but it's a lovely benefit.

Kindness isn't limited to a single behavior. Showing consideration or charity toward another person is something that we can all do. Maybe you already think that you are kind enough, but given the breadth of kindness, we all have the chance to improve.

How hard is it for us to be kind to others? Do you have to know someone to extend your kindness toward them? Being kind doesn't mean giving away all that you have to people in need. Even though I can't meet the financial needs of everyone that crosses my path, I can still smile, be nice, and treat others as though they have value and purpose.

Kindness extends beyond financial giving. One can give generously and still not show kindness. Kindness is about treating someone as though they matter. Kindness is about looking beyond someone's exterior and extending them grace based on them being a human being. Eric Bazilian wrote a song "What if God was One of us" that adds a lot of perspective to this concept. What if God is walking among us on Earth, and what if he was dressed like a homeless person? Not knowing who he was, how would you treat him? Everyone deserves to be treated with respect and kindness.

If someone has no significance in your personal life, does that mean they don't merit kindness? When I think of all of the times someone I didn't know disrespected me or treated me like I didn't matter simply because I had no direct impact on their lives that they knew about, it makes me realize how little we as people actually care about each other. You can care about someone's life or well-being even if they have no direct impact on you. Further, you can care about people even whom you dislike or don't admire because that is how you would want someone to treat you. I am not excusing anyone's bad behavior, but maybe someone has a reason as to why they are surly or bitter. Perhaps it's not about you and it just so happens that you get the short end of the stick. Show kindness to anyone, even when you don't think they deserve it.

Extend kindness to people who you don't know. Extend kindness to people who are hurting. Extend kindness to people who are less fortunate than you. Extend kindness to people who you dislike. Extend kindness to people who are not kind to you. Be kind.

Day 21 – Happiness Takeaways:

1. There are so many ways to extend kindness.
2. Your kindness shouldn't be dependent on any-one else's behavior.
3. Strangers need your kindness too.
4. Do not discriminate when it comes to showing kindness.
5. Treat people the way you want to be treated.

Reflection Questions

- Who is the kindest person in your life?
- How do they show kindness?
- How do they differ from you?
- How can you demonstrate more kindness?
- When have you relied on the kindness of others?

DAY 22

You Don't Have to if You Don't Want to.

"No one can make you play if you don't want to play." – Oscar Robertson

Have you ever supported a cause or given something away because you felt pressured to do so? Maybe you bought something because a sales person was so aggressive and it was easier to say yes instead of facing a confrontation. Do you make decisions for you or for someone else? Are you choosing to maintain things in your life that you don't even like or enjoy? Do you sacrifice to make things happen in your life that you don't even want? Are you living your life to make someone else happy?

When I was a young twenty something I used to go on dates with guys that I wasn't interested in just because I didn't want to say no. I thought "no" was offensive. In other areas of my life I was better at saying no, but I really struggled in my dating life. For years I engaged in relationships all because it was easier for me to say yes, than to endure rejecting someone or confronting them.

Eventually I grew up and realized that it was okay to say no. You don't have to spend time doing things you don't want to do. You don't have to spend your time with people who make you feel badly about yourself. You don't have to waste time doing work that you don't want to do. What would happen for your life if you took your energy that you put toward doing things that you don't want to do, to actually doing things that you want to do? How much more could your career thrive if you were actually doing something that you wanted?

My pastor told a funny story about everyone in a service he attended giving a large offering because they were pressured to. He was the only person that didn't give. He was extremely giving in nature, but he didn't appreciate being pressured into giving. It turned out that most of the people who did give, did so because they felt pressured. No one wanted to be negatively judged for not giving, so they all gave because they didn't want to be outsiders. What is the merit or value of giving if you give begrudgingly? There is no blessing in the gift.

The idea that we have to live our lives doing things that we don't want to do is just not true. You are allowed to set boundaries and standards for what you will and won't do. Do you have a relationship that you want to continue, but you don't want things to go on as they have been? You have options. You can work on your relationship. You can work to make it better. You can approach the person that you are in a relationship with, be it a family member or a spouse, and you can express that things need to change. You don't have to continue as things are if you don't want to.

There will be times in all of our lives where we do things that we don't want to. It can't be avoided totally; however, if you hate doing something, exert energy toward something that you do like. Perhaps you need to work out, but you hate going to the gym. Instead of complaining about going to the gym, exert energy toward finding some form of physical exercise that you actually do enjoy. There have been many seasons of my life, where I didn't want to go to work. I mean I absolutely dreaded going. I had bills to pay and a lifestyle that I wanted to sustain. As I wasn't in a financial position to live without working, and I wasn't comfortable quitting my job at that time, I went to work. In the meantime I exerted energy toward creating a lifestyle that incorporated work that I liked.

The point is to make sure that the decisions you make in life have purpose. You shouldn't live a life full of work, relationships, and activities that you dislike and that don't lead you closer to your goals. You also shouldn't live a life full of decisions that are simply made to please someone else. You don't have to be bullied or pressured into giving your time, your money, or giving of yourself. You just don't have to. You will never be happy if every choice or decision you make involves things that you don't want to do.

Is there anything in your life that you don't want to do? Stop doing it and work toward doing things that make you happy. If you can't just stop immediately, begin to make decisions that will set you up so that you don't have to keep doing that thing that you don't want to do. You don't have to continue to live the same life doing things you don't want to do. I repeat; you just don't have to!

Day 22 – Happiness Takeaways:

1. It is okay to say "no."
2. You don't have to do things that you don't want to.
3. You have options.
4. You don't have to accept things as they are.
5. Exert energy toward getting to the place where you can do what you want.
6. You can't enjoy your life doing things that make other people happy, while making yourself unhappy.

Reflection Questions

- How many of the things in your life, are things that you do because you want to?
- How many things do you do because you have to?
- Of the things that you have to do, how many of them do you actually have to do?
- Can you eliminate some of the things that you don't actually have to do?
- What do you accomplish when you do things that you don't want to or have to do?

Day 23

Treat People the Way You Want to be Treated.

"If you treat an individual as if he were what he ought to be and could be, he will become what he ought to be and could be." - Johann Wolfgang von Goethe

Has someone ever spoken to you rudely? Have you ever noticed that when you match such a tone the outcome is not pleasant? I had an email exchange where someone approached me in a disrespectful way and when I replied equally disrespectfully it caused the originator of the email to become angry. I wanted to talk to this guy about a disagreement we were having, and so I asked him in the email when he was free to talk on the phone. I much prefer to resolve issues face to face or over the phone. He replied to my email saying that he had no interest in talking to me and would prefer to limit our interaction to email. I explained to him that he was the rudest person that I knew, and eventually I picked up the phone and told him a few more of my thoughts. I knew exactly what the person was thinking at the time. "How could she talk to me like that?" There are far too many bullies and self-centered people in our society. It amazed me that this person thought it was perfectly fine to disrespect me, yet he didn't receive it too well when I retaliated. If he would have stopped to ask himself one critical question the entire exchange would have been avoided.

"How would I feel if someone said this to me, in that way?"

I admit that matching his behavior was maybe not the best solution, especially since that didn't actually resolve anything and it didn't positively impact his behavior toward me in the future. What I should have done was be the bigger person. I shouldn't have allowed him to bring me down to his level.

While you shouldn't let people walk all over you, you should not reflect someone's negative energy back to them. If someone projects their issues and rudeness onto you, you don't have to react back in the same way. Rise above that person's behavior. I am not suggesting that you let people slap you around and verbally abuse you. I'm simply saying that because someone is rude to you, that doesn't mean you have to be rude in return. You are planting the same seeds that they are if you do so. Do not let someone impact the harvest that you receive in your life.

It is easy to get caught up in our feelings when most of our worlds focus on "I" or "me." The norm in our society is to focus on our own advancement and success outside of a concept of a community. I have found it shocking and surprising how lacking the concept of "team" has been in my career. I have seen far too many women and men seeking promotion by sacrificing someone else.

Unfortunately, I don't really believe that there is a simple way to fix this societal problem of ours. How do you make people care about others or see themselves as being just one piece of the puzzle, instead of seeing their life as the entire puzzle? Though we are all guilty of being self-centered at times in our lives, it is critical that we consciously treat people in the same manner that we want to be treated.

What separates your life from someone who you think is much worse off than you? In recently trying economic times that have had a global impact, it is important for us all to remember that nothing is promised to us. You and your family could lose your job or your home. A natural disaster or illness could very easily erase everything that you have in just an instant. If you had nothing, how would you want to be treated? If you struggled with addiction and couldn't find the strength to overcome, how would you want to be treated?

Or what if you were going through a divorce or were dealing with a child heading down the wrong path in life? How would you want to be treated? Sometimes people are dealing with things that are unknown to us. Treating people the way you want to be treated is a step toward planting the right seeds. If you treat people awfully you will find that people don't really care about you in return. If you are generous and kind there won't be anything that someone won't do for you.

Take a step back and reflect on the different areas of your life; work, family, social or professional organizations, spiritual, and your community. How do you treat people? You will not be happy without treating people in the same manner that you desire of others; with kindness and integrity. Until you treat all people in the appropriate way, you will continue to feel mistreated.

In my example with my colleague I wasn't the originator, but being rude back surely doesn't reflect how I want people to treat me. It's a very simple concept to implement into your life; treat people the way you want to be treated. Before you act, make sure that your behavior mirrors how you would want someone to treat you.

Day 23 – Happiness Takeaways:

1. Don't treat someone poorly even if they deserve it.
2. Don't allow someone's bad energy to impact your behavior.
3. Give someone a break, as you are human and you have your bad days too.
4. You don't always know exactly what someone is going through.

Reflection Questions

- Do you always treat people the way you want to be treated?
- What are the three most important things that you want from others?
- If someone doesn't treat you the way you want to be treated, how do you react?
- How can you improve your response to being mistreated or misunderstood?

DAY 24

Practice.

**"Practice is the best of all
instructors." – Publilius Syrus**

Babies come into the world unable to do anything for themselves. They don't come out of the womb walking and talking. First they must be able to hold up their heads. Eventually they develop the strength to sit up on their own. From there they start crawling and standing. They take steps and they fall. They wobble and lose their balance. When they actually start walking, they don't master it instantaneously.

I was so hard on myself at one point in my life because I really struggled letting go of something. Everyone knows that saying, "if you love something set it free…if it doesn't come back to you it was never yours, but if it comes back it was meant to be." Well I've heard that saying countless times, and it didn't make me feel better at all. Letting go of this particular idea was such a struggle for me. Then one day, I had an epiphany when I reflected on a baby learning to walk.

Change and growth are not events. Physical changes that take place as a result of working out take three to four weeks before you see results. It is true for breaking bad habits or establishing new habits as well. Just as it doesn't take one minute to form a bad habit, it doesn't take one minute to eliminate such habits. Some people gain weight over time, yet they get frustrated and upset when they can't lose a lot of pounds in a short period of time. It takes time to see the results of your behavior adjustment.

You can change your mind set in one minute, but you won't experience results immediately. The key is that you keep trying and that you hold on to your goals. Take things one day at a time. Patience, persistence, practice, and diligence are essential to following through.

You can't be so hard on yourself that you give up. Failure is part of the process, and though you shouldn't necessarily plan for it, you should not beat yourself up if you fall off the wagon. Fighting through failure is critical. You can't advance if you don't master what it is you are trying to accomplish or change. If you give up without putting in the work and practice, you will never be happy. You will have regrets and you will always wonder "what if."

Remember when you were a child learning how to add and subtract? You counted on your fingers and drew little sticks and added them up. Now many years later addition is no big deal. What took you minutes to figure out, you know instantly without even thinking about it. Now consider when you were learning multiplication. I thought I was such a rock star when I was learning how to multiply. Now when I multiply in my head, I don't really give myself much credit. Things that are difficult initially get easier over time.

I used to go to the gym in the morning and I would meet up with a group of guys that were extremely hard core about their work outs. When I watched them I was so overwhelmed and intimidated. "There is no way that I can do that," I would think to myself. Eventually I joined them for the most challenging workouts I had experienced in my life. I persevered, and though it was always tough for me, I eventually could hang. It never became "easy" but I was able to do the entire class. The more I attended and went through the work outs, the stronger I became.

Life isn't about being easy. It isn't about being great at something on your first try. If you practice and are diligent, you will improve, and if you stick to it you will become the best that you can be at what it is that you are trying to accomplish. Practice makes things possible, continued practice leads to your perfection.

Day 24 – Happiness Takeaways:

1. It takes time to master anything.
2. It is a process to make or break habits. Not an event.
3. Failure is part of the process of improving.
4. Fight through failure.

Reflection Questions

- How often do you practice your craft?
- Do you procrastinate when it is time to practice?
- How much work do you need to put in to improve?
- How much practice will it take for you to be an expert?
- Can you improve without practice?

DAY 25

Listen to Your Heart.

"The invisible intelligence that flows through everything in a purposeful fashion is also flowing through you." – Wayne Dyer

Since I was a child, I could hear the sound of my inner voice speaking to me. There have been many minor decisions that I made over time based on that voice; go left instead of right, go speak to that stranger, or even avoid doing that thing I wanted to do. There were other times where the voice told me not to do something. When I was in a hurry to buy my first place, my inner voice told me not to but I did anyway and it has been the source of a lot of grief in my life. If only I had listened.

The regrets that we have in our lives aren't from when we did or didn't take certain actions. The regrets we have are based on us hearing that voice in our heart speaking very clearly and not following it. Those are the decisions that we make and regret. I heard a woman tell a story of walking down the aisle to meet her fiancé at the altar. She very clearly heard her inner voice say "don't do it." How do you end an engagement as you are walking down the aisle? She'd spent so much money and her family and friends were all present. She chose to make a decision that she knew was wrong instead of risking embarrassment and financial loss. The marriage didn't last. Would you knowingly make the wrong decision, because it's the easier one to make?

I never want to look at my life and realize that I didn't do something because I got in my own way. I don't want to ever say, "Wow I didn't listen to myself, and as a result I didn't fulfill my purpose." I don't want to miss out because I listened to the voice of someone besides myself. If I make a decision that pans out terribly, let it be because I followed my voice, which I don't think would actually happen because your inner voice won't misguide you.

Who knows you better than you know yourself? Who knows your secrets and your intimate thoughts? Who knows how you really feel? Why is it sometimes easier to deny ourselves, listening to our own voices? Why do you feel better about the answer someone else gives you rather than your own answer? When I was younger I didn't feel comfortable making important decisions and now I don't mind at all. I trust myself.

Life is not static, it is forever changing. You can't be afraid to trust yourself. If you make a decision that ends up being unfavorable, you can make changes. You don't have to "live with it." We have a misconception that we will be forced to live with the decisions we make forever. What if you change your mind? There are consequences to our actions and decisions, but you always have the opportunity to make changes to impact your life.

Do you seek advice from people before you take time to really understand your feelings about something? Why do we reach out to others instead of trying to get in touch with ourselves and our inner voices? Why would you rather hear from someone else instead of yourself? Take some time and figure out what you think. Not what your parents think, or your friends, or your spouse. What does your Spirit say regarding the matter?

I don't advise against seeking counsel from other people overall, but you need to look inside of yourself and figure out where you stand and what you want before you reach out to someone else. You can't live your life based solely on the wants and needs of others. What do you want? What do you think? What is your inner voice saying? Listen to that voice and follow it.

Day 25 – Happiness Takeaways:

1. Connect with how you really feel.
2. Don't try to figure out how you feel based on what someone else has to say about your feelings.
3. It is okay to change your mind.
4. You don't have to "live" with your decisions.

Reflection Questions

- Can you hear the voice of your heart?
- Do you listen to it when it speaks?
- What outside influences are you listening to?
  - Which are credible influences?
  - Which should you give less value to?
- Do you take time to connect with yourself and your feelings?

DAY 26

Give.

**"But if anyone has the world's goods
and sees his brother in need, yet closes
his heart against him, how does God's
love abide in him?" – 1 John 3:17**

My mother is the most generous person I know. She believes any financial increase she has ever gotten in life can be used to benefit someone else. She gives money so freely to people without much reservation. If she can address someone's financial need she does. As a result, she has never lacked anything in her life. Even in times of financial stress, my family has always had people who would give to meet our needs, in the same way that my mother always has done for others. She doesn't talk about it or make a big deal about it. I only know because I have watched and admired her life. Her life overflows with happiness and joy because she is generous.

A few years ago, I was at the airport waiting for several hours to meet my best friend as we were taking a trip together. A lady asked me for money to check her bags. I was slightly caught off guard because this never happened to me before at an airport. She didn't realize she would need money to do so and she had an empty wallet. She told me that she had watched me for a few hours (I really had been there that long) and it was on her heart to ask me in particular.

I asked her a few questions, knowing I would give her the money. As she walked away I smiled so largely because I know that if I need something, God makes a way and in that moment I was the avenue used to meet someone's need. How awesome it felt to help someone meet a need. I believe that because I am blessed, God uses me to bless others. It's a lovely cycle. You might read this and wonder "What if that lady spent her day in the airport soliciting money from people?" I had the same thought myself, and really, if she did, I wouldn't have cared. I wouldn't have changed what I did. I had the opportunity to help someone, and I was reminded that I have enough that I have something left over to give to others.

Do you know people in life who work extremely hard and have accumulated wealth, yet it seems as though all they do is work, and they don't enjoy their wealth? It's like they work and work just to keep working. Everything in their life revolves around their job and their possessions. There is nothing wrong with working hard, but when you are generous you don't live to work, and you aren't consumed with making more money just to keep it or invest it in your own family or your own life.

Generosity is what adds fulfillment to your life. If you give, you create room in your life to receive. How can you gain more, if you never get rid of some of what you have? How do you receive more in your life? You give more. Every year I clean my closet. I often give away new items or things in really good condition. I sometimes give away things that I can still wear and want to wear. But I realize I have more than I need and that someone else can benefit from what I have.

When I give cheerfully and without hesitation, I make room in my life to receive the things for which I've believed for. The more you give the more room you have left to receive.

Day 26 – Happiness Takeaways:

1. You have more than enough, so give some away.
2. Don't let making money consume you.
3. Free up space to receive by giving.
4. Find fulfillment in giving to others.
5. You can be generous no matter how much money you have.

Reflection Questions

- Is there someone that you know that can benefit from your generosity?
- What can you give to them to help meet their needs?
- Is there an organization that needs your financial support that you can help?
- Are there people in your life in financial need that you can pray for?
- Can you set aside a certain amount every month to give to someone in need?
- What can you afford to give besides money?

DAY 27

Don't Rely on Someone Else for Your Own Happiness.

"Happiness depends on ourselves." – Aristotle

Being in love is one of the greatest feelings in the world to me. I believe that sharing love with others is a beautiful thing. As much joy as I have experienced in relationships, I have also felt an enormous amount of sadness or loss when they've ended. It was as though a part of me died when a particular relationship ended. At times in my past I relied on relationships with men to make me happy. Thus, when the relationships ended, so did my happiness.

No matter how great relationships are, be them familial, platonic, or romantic, we can't rely on others to be our source of happiness. As we are human, so are the other people in our lives. It is not the job of someone else to make you happy, the same way that you are not responsible for someone else's happiness. Loved ones contribute to our happiness, but it is not the responsibility of anyone to make you happy. As hard as I try to be a source of joy for my loved ones, sometimes I fail. I am human and often I disappoint people. It is not up to me to keep you happy.

When we form a bond with someone, even in the most intimate ways, we create ties and connections but never do we connect in a permanently physical way. Having one mind and body with someone doesn't actually mean that we literally share a mind and body with them. For example, when we engage in sexual intercourse, we are as physically connected as two people can be, but we don't stay physically connected forever. We eventually separate and at the end of the day, what resulted in two bodies becoming one returns to two separate bodies.

The bonds that we create with other people are beautiful and lovely, and while we feel that people can become part of us, we are still separate. No matter how much you love someone, you do not physically share thoughts. That person can't get inside of your body and brain, and they can't physically control your limbs. They can't read your mind or experience life in the same way that you do from your perspective.

No matter how close you are to someone, they don't always know the right thing to do or say to you. Even our closest loved ones hurt and disappoint us. That is part of life. We hurt and disappoint people too, whether we try to or not. How can we hold our loved ones responsible for our happiness? It's not fair to them. You are responsible for your actions and for your happiness. While we expect certain things from our loved ones, we can't rely on them to be the source of our happiness.

I remember going through a break up with a guy that I loved so deeply. We called it quits for about the fourth time, and though I didn't see how things could work out I really wanted to be with him. I felt such a loss when I wasn't connected to him. When we stopped talking I went through days of feeling depressed and unhappy.

When we were together he would text me to have a great day or ask me how my day was going. He would tell me how pretty he thought I was and express how he missed me. In a sense, I started to rely on him to affirm me in certain ways, and without his affirmations, I felt unsure about myself.

There is nothing wrong with expecting someone to do certain things, but what happens if they stop? Are you suddenly unhappy? What if your loved one passes away? Where does that leave you? Is your life over too? In the midst of love and relationships it is key that we sustain our identities and constantly remember that though we appreciate others and the beauty that they add to our lives, that even if we are alone, or even if people disappoint or let us down, we can still be happy.

We can't define our happiness through the actions of others. Doing so is not sustainable, nor is it fair to others around us. It is not healthy to think, feel, and live based on how others treat us or how others behave. When I was at my lowest, I had to ask myself if I would remain depressed if no one ever came into my life and replaced the man that I lost. While I didn't expect that to be the case, I had to understand that no matter what goes on in life, I am responsible for my actions and my happiness.

When we let the actions and behaviors of others dictate our feelings, we spend a lot of time reacting. Our boss is having a good day, and treats us well therefore we have a good day. Our partner is stressed out, therefore we are stressed out. Our children are disobedient, therefore we are unhappy. Our parents are in good health, therefore we are happy. Our neighbors finally mowed their lawn, so today is a good day.

Though others impact your story, they do not control who you are or how you feel. No matter what is going on with your boss, partner, children, parents, or neighbors, you can still make choices that enhance and benefit your life. It is not up to anyone else to make you happy. It is up to you.

Day 27 – Happiness Takeaways:

1. It's not someone's job to make you happy.
2. If you rely on other people to make you happy you will be on an endless emotional rollercoaster.
3. Don't put the burden of your emotions on someone else.
4. Take responsibility for your own happiness.

Reflection Questions

- What makes you happy?
- Who makes you happy?
- What if you didn't have that person or those people in your life?
  - Would you be able to be happy otherwise?
- Were you happy before knowing that person?
- How can you learn to be happy without regard to the behavior of your loved ones?

DAY 28

Cheer for Yourself.

"To be a champ you have to believe in yourself when nobody else will." – Sugar Ray Robinson

When I was a senior in high school, I ran to be our senior class vice president. My best friend and I decided she would be president and I would be vice president. I remember the day that we were set to give our campaign speeches to our classmates. Though that was so many years ago, I have very vivid memories of walking on stage and preparing to present my speech. I will never forget how it felt to get booed in front of my peers. Yes, booed. It wasn't everyone but there were a few for sure. One of the school administrators wanted me to stop giving my speech and I was so upset. "Why should I stop giving my speech because I'm being booed?" I ignored him and the people booing me, and I finished my speech. I did it with such flair and elegance that some of my classmates took note, and congratulated me for how I handled the situation. I had to give another speech at graduation, and I slightly expected a rude classmate or two to embarrass themselves by booing again, but it didn't happen.

Despite the experience, which was pretty major for a 17 year-old high school girl, I never let the memory impact me regarding public speaking. To be honest, though I will never forget what happened, the experience doesn't come to mind when I have to speak. I was able to have a great perspective in recognizing that my classmates were ignorant, and their rude behavior had nothing to actually do with me.

I've had countless experiences in life where I knew that others around me didn't want me to succeed. I know that people aren't always out to get me, but sometimes people just don't expect or want me to win. Can you relate? Maybe their thoughts are based on you having bad behavior in the past. Or maybe competitors of yours want you to fail so that they can win. Maybe people are too preoccupied with their own lives to give you the support that you need or desire. The point is that we can't always rely on others to cheer for us. While we will likely always have someone in our corner, it is important for us to learn to be our biggest cheerleaders.

You can't be defeated just because you don't have a huge crowd of supporters in your corner. There will always be naysayers. It is essential that we believe in ourselves and cheer for ourselves, whether someone else does or not. If everyone else expects you to fall on your face, instead of letting their doubt discourage you, let it fuel you. If no one has the faith to believe in you, let your faith in yourself be enough.

In the times in my life when I didn't have a group of people booing for me or waiting for me to fail, I often served that purpose myself. It's all too easy for us to be our own worst critic than for us to be our biggest cheerleader. One day I confided in a coworker how inefficient I felt because I wasn't accomplishing things fast enough in life. I could clearly see where I wanted to be in life, but I spent more energy planning and talking about the next steps than actually taking action. I was down on myself that day and I directed a lot of criticism and judgment internally. After my friend listened she pointed out to me that while there are areas I could improve upon for sure, I had a lot to be proud of thus far.

That day after lunch I had a conversation with a colleague. He told me that he had just raved about my work to another colleague and he expressed how enjoyable it was for him to work with me, and also that he respected how hard I work and how much effort I put into things. When we got off the phone I was shocked, not because I didn't believe the things that he said, but because his view of me was so far different from the view I had expressed of myself earlier in the day.

Often times we view ourselves from a lens that includes the view of our future selves. Instead of appreciating who we are today and celebrating ourselves, we focus on all the things that we haven't done, without recognizing all that we have already accomplished. You may need to work harder and longer to get to where you want, but acknowledge your strengths today more than your weaknesses. Honor who and where you are today. Celebrate your journey thus far. We should always strive to be better and to reach further; however, doing so doesn't mean that we have to invalidate the greatness that already lies within us.

I have a long way to go, but I've also come a long way. While I'm on my journey, it is okay for me to recognize that I'm pretty cool today. You are awesome, and the brightness of your present will guide you toward your future. Be encouraged and instead of being your worst critic, become your best cheerleader. Don't beat yourself up hoping that will advance your progress. Seek inspiration instead. Make sure to balance your tough love with encouragement. You must cheer for yourself no matter what.

Day 28 – Happiness Takeaways:

1. Everyone is not cheering for you and that is okay.
2. When no one else believes in you, keep believing in yourself.
3. Don't let the doubt of others overshadow your belief.
4. Don't be your biggest critic.
5. Be your biggest fan.
6. You are awesome and amazing.

Reflection Questions

*   What is your theme song that gets you pumped?
*   What is your power color that inspires you?
*   What is your quote or affirmation that you refer to?
*   Who are the members of you pep squad?

DAY 29

Forgive.

**"The weak can never forgive. Forgiveness is
the attribute of the strong." – Mahatma Gandhi**

Does anyone else struggle to forgive, or is it just me?

When a family member or loved one behaves in a
way that hurts you it's not always easy to shake off the
negative feelings or emotions. It's even worse when you
weren't expecting that person to hurt you. When someone has a history of questionable behavior or causing
you injury, it's not shocking and when it's expected,
you can brace for the impact. But when you are totally
caught off guard and unprepared, recovering can take
some time.

A few years ago I dealt with a situation where
someone in my family made me really angry. I of course
learned a great lesson from the situation, and I vowed
that I would never put myself in a similar situation to
be hurt. I would never give that person or anyone the
chance to hurt me again in that same way. Let's fast

forward ahead to the present. I hadn't thought much of that person recently or what transpired because I moved past what happened, or so I thought.

My behavior had been indifferent at best regarding that person; I just stopped caring much about them. But, whenever their name came up I rolled my eyes and I was irritated to even have to think of them. Admittedly, I struggled with disposing of grudges that I've held in the past, but I thought I was bigger than grudges at this point in my life. Saying you have moved past something, even though you actually haven't, doesn't make it real.

I found that my grudge against this person was impacting other relationships in my life. As long as I struggle to forgive someone, how can I expect others to forgive me? I am only human, and while I don't intentionally set out to cause harm to people, I know that I do. Is it fair that we expect to be forgiven without offering forgiveness? Just because you don't speak ill of someone constantly doesn't mean that you aren't harboring a grudge. If you hold ill will against someone in your heart, whether you speak of it or not, you are wrong. Forgive. As this is something that I have struggled with I've had to pray for help to deal with it.

Address the lack of forgiveness that lingers in your heart. As long as it remains, you have less room in your heart for light and loveliness. If you don't have the capacity to forgive, how can others forgive you? As long as your heart holds grudges, there is less room for happiness. Would your rather hold on to a grudge or happiness?

Let the grudge go, today.

Day 29 - Happiness Takeaways:

1. Holding grudges is not healthy for the heart.
2. Replace your grudges with forgiveness.
3. Grudges are heavy and weigh a lot.
4. If you can't forgive someone, you can't expect others to forgive you.

Reflection Questions

- Who do you need to forgive?
- Have you ever communicated your feelings to that person that you have not forgiven?
- How much energy does it take to hold on to your lack of forgiveness?
- In what other ways could you use that energy?
- What will it take for you to forgive?

DAY 30

Love Freely.

"If I speak in the tongues of men and of angels, but have not love, I am only a resounding gong or a clanging cymbal. If I have the gift of prophecy and can fathom all mysteries and all knowledge, and if I have a faith that can move mountains, but have not love, I am nothing. If I give all I possess to the poor and surrender my body to the flames, but have not love, I gain nothing. Love is patient, love is kind. It does not envy, it does not boast, it is not proud. It does not dishonor others, it is not self-seeking, it is not easily angered, it keeps no record of wrongs. Love does not delight in evil but rejoices with the truth. It always protects, always trusts, always hopes, always perseveres." – 1 Corinthians 13:1-7

No matter what I've experienced in life, good or bad, significant or meaningless, I've always been loved. I've had an abundance of love in my life, and I've recognized that as a major blessing. At the end of the day the only things that really matter are the people in our lives and our relationships. Reflect on the definition of love in 1 Corinthians shown above. Love is selfless, and through the face of loss, trial, disappointment, and failure, love still endures. Love is how we remain who we are, and in the midst of varying circumstances, the love we share with others remains constant.

In life we are all working toward achieving success, gaining knowledge, being happy, and overall improving ourselves. All of that is great, but if we pursue life without love in our hearts, our lives are void. Empty. Nothing. Meaningless. If we seek to be good people and to do great things without regard for loving others, then our good works are all in vain. If we claim to love, yet we don't love without regard to ourselves and our own feelings, then we don't truly love. Selfish love is not love at all.

It is obviously very easy to get caught up in the challenges that life presents, but it is imperative we don't lose our hearts. We can't forget the importance of love, as it is so connected to our purpose, because without love, we have nothing. We can never truly be happy if love lacks in our lives. How can we reap a harvest of love if we don't plant any seeds of love? Let your love brighten the lives of those around you. When someone only sees darkness and is in search of the light, let your love be the light that they need.

Day 30 – Happiness Takeaways:

1. A life without love is meaningless life.
2. Love matters more than success and accomplishments.
3. Love joins people together.
4. Without love, we can't be happy.

Reflection Questions

- "Love is patient, love is kind. It does not envy, it does not boast, it is not proud. It does not dishonor others, it is not self-seeking, it is not easily angered, it keeps no record of wrongs. Love does not delight in evil but rejoices with the truth. It always protects, always trusts, valways hopes, always perseveres."
  - How can you exemplify this definition of love in your relationships?
  - How can you share your love with others?

Thank you for reading "One Choice, Choose Happiness." My prayer for you is that you live a happier life filled with more love and light. I hope that sharing my journey has helped you along yours. For daily encouragement, check out my blog at happygirlspeaks. com. I would love to hear from you as I love feedback and sometimes I need encouragement too, so please share your inspirational quotes and stories with me at angela@happylifesolutions.com.

More love!

Ang

About the Author

Angela Victoria is a daughter, sister, and dear friend to many. She currently lives in Milwaukee, but you can find her hanging out in Chicago on most weekends. For more from Angela check out her blog Happy Girl Speaks.

Made in the USA
Middletown, DE
30 July 2015